A Handbook of
Biology Teaching Methods

Mollie Pullan

Oxford University Press

Oxford University Press, Ely House, London W.1.

Glasgow New York Toronto Melbourne Wellington
Cape Town Ibadan Nairobi Dar Es Salaam Lusaka Addis Ababa
Delhi Bombay Calcutta Madras Karachi Lahore Dacca
Kuala Lumpur Singapore Hong Kong Tokyo

Printed in Great Britain at the University Press, Oxford
by Vivian Ridler, Printer to the University

CONTENTS

FOREWORD

FOREWORD

This text is an introduction to methods of biology teaching for students training for work in secondary schools. It also provides a source of tried and tested methods and materials, and includes concise reviews of recent developments in curricula in Britain and overseas. As such it is hoped that the book will also be of use to experienced teachers.

The approach and methods suggested have been found suitable for secondary school biology courses in temperate and in tropical countries. The use of expensive apparatus has been avoided as far as is possible, in an attempt to encourage teachers to use an up-to-date teaching approach even where equipment is in limited supply. There is a short section dealing with the special problems of maintaining biology laboratories in hot and humid climates, and suggestions are made for the use of local living specimens in place of standard 'types' which may have to be imported.

Every teacher develops his own approach to teaching, and it is not implied that the methods suggested in this book are invariably 'the best'. Teaching must be constantly adapted to the needs of a particular group of pupils. However, it is unrealistic to expect students to 'construct a learning situation' and 'train their pupils to ask the right questions', until they themselves have some classroom experience and are no longer solving their own problems of class management and work organization. Thus the book is a starting point from which it is hoped students will adapt and develop their own teaching methods. References in the text suggest further sources of teaching methods, which can be explored and used as the student gains experience in schools. With few exceptions, none of the methods suggested are original. I am indebted to my colleagues and students in several countries who have suggested methods, modifications and materials.

SECTION ONE

BIOLOGY IN THE SCHOOL CURRICULUM

1.1 Why teach biology?

The study of biology offers the opportunity to develop an understanding of scientific method and the ability to understand the living world of which man himself is a part. At the present time, it is vitally important that all human beings learn to appreciate the fundamental principles of their environment. Conservation in all its aspects must be an important topic in any biology course. Man is in the unique position of being an animal able to control his own environment, and his survival depends on how well he does so.

Problems of pollution, overpopulation and the ensuing food and fuel shortages are not new, but are rapidly reaching crisis point. Their solution demands international co-operation on a hitherto unprecedented scale and this in turn depends upon an understanding of the issues involved.

Biology is the least exact of the sciences. Living material is subject to the hazards of disease, population explosion and sudden inexplicable death unknown in the physical sciences. Therein can lie both its difficulties and its fascination. Biology experiments are intrinsically open-ended and a great variety of material with which to work can be found in what appear to be the most inhospitable habitats.

In common with other school subjects, the demands of public examinations have, in the past, made school biology merely an accumulation of facts to be learned. Its application to everyday life had become obscured by a concentration on the learning of these facts rather than investigating the principles which they illustrate. If an outline syllabus for any one of the new courses is compared with that of a traditional syllabus, the factual content is seen to vary little.

Educationists have come to realize that *how* something is taught is as important as *what* is taught. Facts are the raw materials from which ideas are developed, and as such are of great importance. But facts alone are of small value, and it is the task of a teacher to present the right mixture of facts and ideas. Wherever possible they should try to guide their pupils to ask the right questions and seek answers through well designed experiments.

A secondary school biology course must meet the needs of future biology specialists as well as those whose study of the subject will end at school. It must be challenging enough for the exceptionally able and interesting enough for the slower learners. The aim must be to develop
  (i) an interest in, and a respect for, living organisms,
 (ii) an understanding of the way in which they function and interact in a community, and
(iii) a critical approach to observation and experimentation.
It is important to emphasize that there is much that scientists do not yet know or understand, and that scientific theories are being continually modified in the light of new discoveries.

Ambition must be tempered with realism. Biological concepts develop slowly and many pupils will not achieve a high level of understanding by the end of their school course. However, it is important that the biological principles which will affect the pupil's post-school environment are introduced in the school curriculum.

An educated citizen of a developing country must understand the principles of nutrition, land use and pest and disease control in man, in his crops and domestic animals. In all countries alike there must be an understanding of world-wide problems of food supply, population control and conservation.

Biology must not be regarded as a purely utilitarian subject. From the field studies incorporated in the new curricula such interests as photography, painting, mountaineering and other outdoor pursuits may develop. With the growing amount of leisure time available it is important that schools encourage interests which are profitable and in which pupils can be active participants rather than passive spectators.

In industrialized societies an appreciation of the natural environment needs to be preserved and fostered. It is equally important that children growing up in countries which still have a largely rural population learn to appreciate their unspoiled environment. School Biology Clubs can do much to encourage these wider interests and are discussed in a later section.

1.2 Curriculum development

TERMINOLOGY

Integrated approach

In the sciences this implies that the three main branches of science are treated as a single subject. The emphasis is on basic scientific concepts, such as energy relationships, which are important in physics, chemistry and biology. In most respects it is an improved way of teaching general science, a subject that in the past too rarely unified the separate scientific disciplines.

Some schools are now adopting a unified approach to the curriculum as a whole; this is especially true of C.S.E. courses in Britain, and of Primary School courses in many countries. At Secondary School level, an integrated course of study may be devised for a class, for a small group of pupils or for individual pupils. In this last case, organization of the pupils into classes no longer occurs, and teachers take on the role of 'resource personnel' who advise pupils in their studies and guide their use of materials and texts from the school resource centre.

Individual instruction

A course of work is presented so that each pupil can progress at his own rate. Generally there is basic work for all pupils, with additional material for the more able, together with tests. Practical work is an integral part of science courses for the individual pupil.

A recently published biology course entitled *Biology for the Individual*[1] covers the first two years of the secondary school course, and is based on *Nuffield Biology*[2] and *Nuffield Combined Science*[3].

Team teaching

Science teachers are usually trained in two of the three main branches of science; generally biology with chemistry, or chemistry with physics. Integrated science courses should ideally be taught by one teacher qualified in all three scientific subjects and in mathematics, but this is rarely possible. Team teaching provides one solution to this problem. Two or more teachers collectively qualified in physics, chemistry and biology combine their classes and share the teaching. Individual teachers lead pupils in discussion and in design of experiments in their own specialist area, and the rest of the team assist in the supervision of group and individual work. Team teaching demands large, well-equipped laboratories but it does assist in the teaching of large classes of pupils.

Circus

This is a course that consists of a set of experiments, demonstrations and pieces of reading each taking the same amount of time. Groups of pupils progress around the 'circus' until all pieces of work have been completed. A circus may occupy one lesson or a sequence of lessons.

Though this method of teaching takes a considerable time to prepare, the teacher is free during class time to assist with individual difficulties. Once such a set of activities is worked out, it can be used in future with much less preparation time involved.

Route

Many of the new courses are presented as a source for teaching more topics than can possibly be included in the time available. Teachers are expected to select the topics and the sequence of topics that are best suited to their pupils. The chosen sequence is described as a 'route'. Several courses give guidance in 'route finding' by providing summaries of topics and by showing their inter-relationships. (The latter may be termed 'bridges'.)

Programmed instruction

In these courses, each topic is broken down into the smallest possible steps and arranged in the best learning sequence. Individual pupils are able to work through a programmed course at their own rate. Programmes may be in book form or printed on cards. Progress may be controlled by having the steps mechanically presented by teaching machines, with built-in correction of errors. Some programmes include background reading and many incorporate practical work. Of particular interest to biologists are the B.S.C.S. *Patterns and Processes*[5] and the *Programmed Biology Series* from Pitman[4].

NEW COURSES

In recent years practically every country in the world has revised its science teaching methods, and in many cases revolutionized the content of the school syllabi. All new courses have in common a trend away from authoritarian teaching, in which the emphasis is on the learning of facts. An experimental approach to topics relevant to the life of the community is a feature of these courses.

There has been much international co-operation in the development of the new materials, and this is being continued during rewriting and trials in schools. All of the texts and source books discussed below contain relevant teaching matter, wherever one's own school might be. Several of the texts, notably the B.S.C.S. books, *Nuffield Biology* and the *UNESCO Biology Pilot Project,* represent the foundations on which later courses have been built.

Biological science curriculum study

During 1957–58 educationists and biologists from schools, colleges and universities in the United States of America were given the task of devising a course of high-school biology. This was to have a sound scientific basis for future specialists, while also being relevant and interesting to all pupils, whatever their future careers might be.

The American system of education differs from the British and British-influenced systems in that courses are more intensive and of shorter duration. The B.S.C.S. courses are intended for one year of high school (out of a total of four years). The texts are therefore more suitable for senior pupils in secondary schools and as background reading for teachers.

Three courses were developed, approaching the subject from different main concepts. The versions have come to be known as much by the colour of their bindings as by their titles, thus the colloquial names are given below in addition to the full title.

Molecules to Man (Blue Version)[6] is based on molecular biology. The most difficult version, it covers much of the work of the Advanced Level of the General Certificate of Education, and similar examinations.

High School Biology (Green Version)[7] is an ecology-based text, and of the greatest interest to the general reader. It can be used with advantage in sixth form general courses for non-science specialists, being well illustrated and interesting in content.

Biological Science: An Inquiry into Life (Yellow Version)[8] has an evolutionary emphasis. This version has been adapted for the Philippine Islands, and is suitable for countries having a similar tropical fauna and flora. Another adaptation was made at a workshop in India, especially for pre-university course students in Indian Senior High Schools.

The three versions, despite their special emphases, all form a basic course of biology. No topic usually taught in a school course is neglected. The excellent illustrations and clear language make all the three courses especially suitable for background reading for senior pupils whose mother tongue is not English, but who have to study in this language.

There is a Laboratory Manual and a Teachers' Guide for each version. Much of the work is highly structured, and for many schools the practical work suggested will be beyond the facilities available. These were the first courses produced in which pupils are encouraged to investigate for themselves, to formulate generalizations and look for patterns. The work of the B.S.C.S. group continues, and many other materials have been developed in recent years. Of special interest are the following:

1. *Biology Teachers' Handbook* by J.J. Schwab[9] which is a guide to the use of the B.S.C.S. materials, together with the necessary background work in the physical sciences and statistics. Methods of assessment are discussed, and there is a section on the preparation of standard laboratory reagents.

2. *Research Studies in Biology: Investigations for Students*[10]. Of interest to College of Education students about to begin a Special Study in biology, this series of books is a collection of suggestions for research projects of a simple nature, contributed by research biologists. Some of the problems could be investigated by a school biology club.

3. *Laboratory Blocks*. Various topics and authors. Prepared by the Committee on Innovation in Laboratory Instruction, these booklets provide a complete series of laboratory studies in specialized fields. The microbiology block[11] is especially useful.

4. *Patterns and Processes*[4] is a text and teachers' guide for the slower pupil. The text is programmed in the sections which give the essential basic facts. Once the factual knowledge is established, it is used in investigations, and the emerging principles are fully discussed and emphasized. It is a good example of the use of programmed learning.

5. Pamphlets on specialized topics[12] are published frequently, and include results of the latest research. They are a means of keeping

in touch with the latest developments for both teachers and senior pupils.

The influence of the B.S.C.S. materials has been wide. It can be seen in the latest courses developed in countries as diverse as Australia, India and East Africa. Teachers in all parts of the world should therefore be conversant with the three main texts, the laboratory manuals and the teachers' guides.

Nuffield O level biology

First introduced as trial materials for schools in 1962, this five-year course marked the beginning of curriculum reform in the United Kingdom. (Scottish Education Authorities have since produced their own courses.)

It would be unfair to the many teachers who were teaching in a 'Nuffield' way long before this course was developed to suggest that it is new and revolutionary. It does, however, take the best tried and tested methods and incorporates them into a scheme of work covering the Ordinary Level General Certificate of Education.

Not all schools have adopted the course in full (far fewer than is generally supposed in overseas countries), but the effect on biology teaching in general has been profound. The essential difference between 'Nuffield' and 'traditional' biology is that the former poses questions to which pupils are encouraged to find the answers. There is suitable background reading at every stage, and the academic basis is adequate for future specialization in the biological sciences. A Teachers' Guide is provided for each year. As well as describing laboratory techniques, these guides include additional work for the more able pupils.

The success of the course, and its ready acceptance by teachers, is largely due to the fact that all materials were thoroughly tried and tested in normal school situations. Examination boards set special papers for candidates studying Nuffield Biology, and these pupils were, therefore, at no disadvantage in external examinations.

The value of a school curriculum in which authoritarianism is reduced to a minimum, cannot be overstated. Obviously, the less able pupils need more guidance from the teacher, and with any class the teacher remains firmly in charge of proceedings. But pupils must be encouraged to ask questions and initiate discussion so essential to understanding concepts.

It is often thought that the new curricula demand apparatus and laboratory facilities which are beyond the means of schools in many countries. Although the special apparatus suggested is often the most convenient, Nuffield Biology can be taught using the very minimum of equipment. An account of a Nuffield Biology Summer School in India is given in the *Journal of Biological Education*[13], and includes a description of the simple local apparatus used in place of imported, expensive items.

A full account of the essentials of a Nuffield Biology course, including costing of equipment, is given in a pamphlet[14] obtainable free on request from the publishers.

Nuffield combined science

The need for the study of a wide range of subjects during the first two years of a secondary school course does not always enable physics, chemistry and biology to be studied as separate disciplines. Therefore the Nuffield Foundation sponsored the production of a junior science course with an approach similar to that of the 'O' level texts. *Nuffield Combined Science* became available in 1970. Thirty-five trial schools, eighty teachers and over three thousand pupils were involved in the preparation and testing of the materials.

The course consists of ten topics, from the sub-sections of which a teacher is able to select those most suitable for his classes. Two *Teachers' Guide Books* and an *Apparatus Guide* give complete background work and there is a section on route-finding in *Teachers' Guide I.* There are no class text books. *Activities Packs* for pupils are workbooks which give guidance for practical work, its recording and applications.

It is not necessary to provide these books for each pupil, though desirable if the school can afford them. It is possible to teach the work using only the *Teachers' Guides*, though workcards will have to be devised by the teacher for group or individual work.

The suggested timetable allocation is five lessons per week. It is expected that one teacher will teach throughout each year, and the background reading makes this feasible for any science teacher, whatever his specialization. There is no rigid division into the separate sciences, nor are the groupings in any way artificial (as often happened in former 'General Science' subjects). Apart from its classroom use, many topics lend themselves to extended study in Science Clubs.

Nuffield secondary science[15]

Sponsored by the Nuffield Foundation, *Secondary Science* caters for the needs of pupils of average and below-average ability, candidates for the United Kingdom Certificate of Secondary Education rather than the General Certificate of Education. *Working Paper 1*[16] states the aim of this course and realistically assesses the possible achievements.

As in *Combined Science*, there are no class textbooks. The course is arranged as themes, through which routes can be found to provide a sequence and content suited to the needs of classes in differing environments. Suggested routes are given for classes with different interests. It is possible to select a route based on rural studies, on domestic science topics or one relevant to future industrial workers. Much of the work would enrich the teaching of pupils of higher ability, especially in the sections on heredity and evolution, and those dealing with social issues such as drugs, smoking and behavioural studies.

Integrated science

This has recently been developed for pupils of high ability who intend to specialize in arts subjects. These pupils usually have little time to take more than one science subject, and this precludes a change to a science specialization at a later stage.

A suggested lesson allocation of eight or nine lessons per week enables selected topics to be studied in depth. The course is intended to follow early work in *Combined Science* or a similar syllabus. In the biology part this course concentrates on aspects of conservation, world problems of food supply and population, genetics and evolution with the elementary anatomy and morphology necessary to the understanding of fundamental principles.

Curriculum development in developing countries

In recent years there has been an enormous expansion of educational facilities in the developing countries of Africa and Asia. New Primary and Secondary Schools, Colleges and Universities are being founded, often aided by international and bilateral funds and loans. Accompanying the increase in institutions, teaching methods and the content of the curriculum are being revolutionized.

Curriculum improvement in these countries is no easy task. Pupils are bound by economic necessity to pass their external examinations, and there is constant pressure on their teachers to study only material which can be seen as relevant to 'the syllabus', and which is easy to learn by rote. A course in which ideas have to be worked out, and time spent devising experiments can only become popular with pupils and teachers of the countries concerned when examination requirements are changed in accordance with new teaching methods.

In the countries where examination reform has coincided with curriculum changes, progress has been rapid. In others, teachers and pupils are reluctant to try out new methods, feeling that examination success will be jeopardized. There is also a current myth that new teaching techniques demand expensive equipment, and are time-consuming. The production of cheap apparatus kits is countering the former misconception, and in-service training courses for teachers enable many to see that the teacher's attitude to learning is more important than the provision of costly apparatus.[13]

The West African Examinations Council initiated curriculum reform at Advanced Level by a total revision of the syllabus. The Biology syllabus for Nigeria, Ghana, Sierra Leone and the Gambia was completed during 1965—66. It has an ecological bias suited to the needs of biologists in countries where the economy is largely based on agriculture. Revision of the Ordinary Level syllabus followed, though the changes were not so great. Secondary schools in some parts of West Africa have been using the Nuffield Biology O level courses for some years, and Advanced Teacher Training Colleges are augmenting the supply of grammar school teachers by training non-graduates with a modern approach to their work.

In India, the National Council for Educational Research and Training, a government-sponsored organization, is carrying out curriculum reform at all levels. Two biology courses, approximating to the Ordinary Level of the General Certificate of Education, are currently being tested in schools. State Departments of Education are revising syllabi and improving laboratory facilities in the schools under their jurisdiction, and various organizations sponsor in-service training courses for teachers. In a country as diverse as India, it is only to be expected that educational reform will be varied to suit local conditions. However, all new developments are following the international trend of moving away from mere factual learning and towards open-ended experimentation.

East Africa has a School Science Project at the trial stage. Physics, chemistry and biology courses are currently being tested in schools, and examined by the East African Examinations Council. Each course covers the four years of the secondary school course to the equivalent of O level G.C.E. Revision and rewriting of the courses is at an advanced stage. Three organizations have done much to sponsor curriculum renewal in developing countries:

1. United Nations Development Programme

This organization, through the United Nations Educational, Scientific and Cultural Organisation has aided the establishment of Advanced Colleges of Education, whose prime purpose is to train teachers for the first three or four years of the secondary school curriculum.

In addition, the Biology Pilot Project has been developed by U.N.D.P. personnel. This is a course specifically for schools in Africa using local materials and designed for only limited laboratory facilities. Begun in the English-speaking countries, it is now being extended to the French-speaking areas. College, university and school teachers worked together in the production of the course, and therein is the key to its effectiveness.

2. The British Council

The British Council has established science officers in many countries. Assisting scientific development in general, they have also been responsible for introducing Nuffield science courses into countries as diverse geographically and culturally as India and parts of Latin America. The Council, together with the United Kingdom Overseas Development Administration, sponsors in-service training in numerous countries. Their main contribution is the supply of tutors, equipment and books.

3. The Centre for Educational Development Overseas

CEDO was inaugurated in April 1970 by the Minister of Overseas Development. It combines the activities of the pre-existing Centre for Curriculum Renewal and Educational Development Overseas (CREDO), the Overseas Visual Aids Centre (OVAC) and the Centre for Educational Television Overseas (CETO). The organization is non-profit making and independent, although it receives grants from the British government and certain foundations, and works in co-operation with the Overseas Development Administration, the British Council and the British

Broadcasting Corporation. To quote from the organization's brochure 'CEDO will help countries, on request, to realize educational development along lines desired, approved and needed by the countries themselves'.

The three organizations which formed the nucleus of the new Centre have organized in-service training, workshops and conferences in Britain and overseas. They also provide specialists for specific assignments in educational development. These activities are being continued, together with the development of work in examinations and testing.

The Centre is a clearing house for information in all aspects of educational development, and has a library of textbooks, syllabi, curriculum material, films and filmstrips, together with equipment from all over the world. Teachers departing overseas and teachers visiting Britain may use the library, and the centre states that 'Information and advice will be available through correspondence, publications, lectures and the reception of visitors'. Teachers overseas wishing for information should first contact the local British Council office.

Most of these new curricula incorporate the relevant parts of the Biological Sciences Curriculum Study courses, the Nuffield O levels and the UNESCO Pilot Project materials. Thus it can be seen that biology curriculum reform is international in its sources and yet well adapted to local needs.

SOURCES OF INFORMATION

1. Local Education Authorities

Inspectors and Organizers are often regarded by teachers as senior officers whose sole function is criticism. In fact the local inspectorate is generally the best source of information on curriculum changes, laboratory planning and advice on the suitability of new equipment and apparatus.

Inspectors often organize weekend or evening courses on special aspects of teaching, and welcome suggestions from teachers for useful topics. Where there is a Teachers' Centre, the inspectorate work closely with the staff. Libraries for textbooks, teachers' books, journals and other relevant literature are kept at these centres and publishers and manufacturers frequently hold exhibitions of books in print, new apparatus and materials.

2. Vacation Courses

The Ministry of Education and Universities and Institutes of Education organize extended vacation courses. Local Authorities usually contribute towards the expenses of teachers selected to attend, and the Ministry publish an annual booklet of 'Short Courses for Teachers' in good time for applications to be made. A booklet of 'Long Courses for Teachers' is also produced.

3. Association for Science Education

This national association has branches in most areas of the United Kingdom. Their journal, School Science Review, is published three times a year and is a valuable source of new ideas, book reviews, apparatus, news and correspondence. Students may join the association at a reduced rate, and the annual subscription includes the cost of the journal. Further information can be obtained from the Secretary at College Lane, Hatfield, Herts.

4. School Natural Science Society

Formerly the School Nature Study Union, this society is mainly of interest to primary school teachers, though their publication 'Natural Science in Schools' contains many topics suitable for Science Club activities.

The address of the society is 8, Sandy Lane, Sevenoaks, Kent.

5. Field Studies Council

The Council has residential centres throughout the British Isles. Courses are organized by the staff of the centre, or by teachers who take a group of pupils or students. Most centres specialize in biology and geography, and are located in ecologically interesting areas.

Demand for places always exceeds availability, and it is necessary for the school to join the Council. The offices of the Council are at 9, Devereux Court, London, S.W.1.

6. Youth Hostels' Association

Several Youth Hostels welcome groups of school pupils, with their teachers, for extended stays in one hostel. Some hostels provide suitable work rooms, though most equipment must be taken. Parties take the usual share of domestic work in the hostel, and are naturally most welcome out of the main holiday seasons.

Further information is obtainable from the Y.H.A. offices in Welwyn Garden City, Herts.

7. Institute of Biology

Membership of the Institute is open to biology graduates and to others by examination. The Institute publishes the Journal of Biological Education, specifically concerned with the teaching of the biological sciences. It also sponsors textbooks, for example, the 'Studies in Biology' series published by Edward Arnold, and suitable for Advanced level work for G.C.E.

Student membership of the association costs only 50p per annum. The address of the institute is 41, Queen's Gate, London, S.W.1.

8. British Social Biology Council

Mainly concerned with the application of biology to the social environment, the Council publishes 'Biology and Human Affairs'. Individuals or schools may join the Council, whose offices are at 66, Eccleston Square, London, S.W.1.

Overseas countries

Most countries have a national association of science teachers, and local associations can be formed by groups of interested teachers. The West African and the Indian association publish their own journals, as do the associations in several other countries. The Inspectorate should be able to put teachers in touch with the national secretaries. One day conferences, science exhibitions and vacation courses are often organized.

Institutions particularly concerned in curriculum development may be government organizations or, in larger countries, state controlled. India has a National Council for Educational Research and Training, and the various State Education Authorities have their own Institutes of Education. In other countries the University Education Departments, and Institutes of Education attached to Universities are generally concerned with curriculum research and renewal.

British Council offices usually have a science officer on their staff, able to supply information and advice on the Nuffield Foundation courses. The Council, in conjunction with the United Kingdom Overseas Development Administration sponsor vacation courses. The film library usually has a stock of scientific films and other teaching aids, and copies of the Nuffield Texts are available in the library.

1.3 Science Clubs

A Science Club can be a useful addition to classroom teaching in any school, especially where apparatus and laboratory facilities are limited. Keen pupils are able to carry out their own investigations under the guidance of a teacher not hampered by the need to maintain the interest of a large class.

Preferably a teacher acts as a guide rather than as a controller of club activities. It is of benefit to pupils if a committee is elected from and by the members. It is better to have a relatively small number of interesting and well organized meetings, rather than frequent meetings of less interest.

Possible activities are numerous, including:

1. Designing and carrying out investigations from questions which arise in class time, but are not of interest for the majority—or for which there is not time during normal classroom teaching.
2. Ecological investigations in the school compound or nearby habitats. Records kept over a number of years form a valuable reference source. In the developing countries, where many organisms are not yet identified, there is vast scope for school work in local ecology. Museums and University Departments will assist with identification, and schools could profitably devise simple keys to identification and, more important, descriptions of the organisms.
3. Visits to places of interest such as forestry plantations, blood donor services, dairies, manufacturers of foods and drugs have an added value in giving information on possible careers.
4. Film shows and talks by outside speakers.
5. Talks and demonstrations of experiments by pupils.

The most valuable activities are those in which the pupils participate. Experiments, collections and pieces of apparatus made by pupils can be entered in the competitions frequently organized by science associations and education authorities. Should there be no national or regional competitions, a school one can be arranged, and will do much to stimulate interest in the club.

Special biological interests can be catered for by a Biology or Natural History Club, or there may be participation in the activities of a club covering all branches of science. Much depends on the numbers involved and the range of interests.

Some countries have national associations to which school clubs can be affiliated. Kenya, for example, has a national organization of Wildlife Clubs, with its headquarters in the National Museum. The objectives are to further the interest of the coming generation in the country's wildlife, which is an important tourist attraction and hence a source of revenue. The economy of the country depends very much on conservation of its relatively unspoiled rural areas.

School Clubs should be concerned with biological education in its widest sense—the development of an awareness of the importance of biology in the environment.

Bibliography

1. Reid, D.J. and Booth, P.   Biology for the Individual.   Heinemann.

    1. Sorting animals and plants into groups 1970
    2. How life begins   1970
    3. Movement in animals   1970
    4. Support in animals and plants   1971
    5. The problems of life in hot and cold climates   1971
    Other titles are forthcoming.

2. Biology.   Nuffield Foundation

    Text I   Introducing Living Things
    Teachers' Guide I
    Text II Life and Living Processes
    Teachers' Guide II
    Text III The Maintainence of Life
    Teachers' Guide III
    Text IV Living Things in Action
    Teachers' Guide IV
    Text V The Perpetuation of Life
    Teachers' Guide V

    Longmans/Penguin Books 1966

3. Combined Science. Nuffield Foundation
   Teachers' Guide I
   Teachers' Guide II
   Teachers' Guide III
   Activities Pack I
   Activities Pack II
   Longmans/Penguin Books 1970

4. Programmed Biology Series. Pitman
   Titles include:
   Teachers' Manual
   Mitosis and Meiosis
   D.N.A.: The Key to Life
   The Structure and Function of the Cell
   The above titles by Gary Parker, W. Ann Reynolds and Rex Reynolds

   Energy Organisation and Life. R. Rodrigo Panares
   Introduction to Chemistry for Biology Students.
                                        George I. Sackheim
   Genes and Population. Paul Geisert

5. Biological Science Patterns and Processes:
   B.S.C.S. Text and Teachers' Guide
   Holt, Rinehart and Winston   1963

6. Biological Science: Molecules to Man
   B.S.C.S. Blue Version
   Houghton Mifflin Co, Boston
   Edward Arnold (Publishers) Ltd., London

7. High School Biology
   B.S.C.S. Green Version
   Rand McNally and Co. Chicago

8. Biological Science: An Inquiry into Life
   B.S.C.S. Yellow Version
   Harcourt Brace and World, New York

9. Biology Teachers' Handbook. J.J. Schwab, Supervisor
      John Wiley and Sons, N.Y. and London

10. Research Studies in Biology: Investigations for Students. B.S.C.S.
       Doubleday & Co, New York

11. Microbes: their growth, nutrition and interaction. A.S. Sussman
       D.C. Heath & Co. Boston   (B.S.C.S. text)

12. B.S.C.S. Pamphlet Series
      D.C. Heath, Boston

13. J. Biol. Ed. (1971) 5, 173–177   J.R. Parry Williams & Mollie
                                                                    Pullan
       On the Adaptation of Indian Teachers to a Short Course on
       Nuffield Biology.

14. The Nuffield Foundation Science Teaching Project
       Biology pamphlet published for the Nuffield Foundation by
                                        Longman/Penguin Books 1968

15. Secondary Science. Themes 1–7, Teachers' Guide and
                                                            Apparatus Guide
       Longman/Penguin 1971

16. Working Paper No. 1 (produced for the Nuffield Foundation
                                           Teaching Project) 1965
       Free in the U.K. from the Schools Council.

17. Patterns. Pupils' Books 1–4   Teachers' Guides 1–4
       Technicians' Manual 1–4   Topic Books
       Longman/Penguin 1973

See also: Useful Addresses for Science Teachers. Edward Arnold
                (U.K. only)

PLANNING AND TEACHING A COURSE OF BIOLOGY

2.1 Interpreting the syllabus

Teachers are often required to take a middle course between teaching as they think best and teaching for examination success. Examination reform in recent years has done much to resolve this conflict, though it still exists in many countries.

In fairness to those who prepare examination syllabi, it must be stated that they are usually prepared with broad educational aims in view. The narrowing, which so often comes about, is due both to teachers who concentrate on rote learning and neglect to develop understanding of basic principles by their pupils, and to the type of examination papers set. Too often, a good memory is the main criterion of success.

Teachers who present work as problem-solving situations and who seek to develop an understanding of basic concepts, find that their pupils achieve a high level of success in any type of examination. Most teachers now favour an experimental, open-ended teaching method, and it is essential that, at every stage of work, the ideas and basic facts are clearly given and discussed. Failure to discuss and summarize work with the class is one reason why many new courses have fallen into disrepute. None of the new-style courses suggest that facts are unnecessary—they are, after all, the raw materials from which ideas are developed. It is unrealistic to suggest that it is never necessary to sit down and learn facts. What is important is that what is learned is seen to be relevant to the formulation of concepts, and necessary to their full understanding.

The essential requirements for interpreting the syllabus with both educational aims and examination success in mind are:

1. Decide what necessary facts are required.
2. Identify those facts which can be explained by experiment in the classroom and those which must be accepted.
3. Add any additional material, not indicated on the syllabus, which is needed for interest and/or understanding.

This is obviously a compromise, but one which few teachers are in a position to ignore, until there is something of a revolution in many school curricula and, more particularly, in the examination techniques which are used.

It is helpful, particularly with classes of high ability, to explain the sources of new scientific knowledge. Although journals such as *Nature* and *Scientific American* are inappropriate for reading until Advanced level, a glance through them gives an indication of how research results are made available. A visit to a university library is certainly appropriate for sixth form pupils.

2.2 Planning a scheme of work

A scheme of work is a forecast of the type of work to be covered in a specified time, together with an indication of the teaching methods to be used. A scheme may be designed for the whole of a G.C.E. course, or for the few weeks of a teaching practice. It is not a rigid plan, and can be altered with experience, the rate of progress of a class and the need to incorporate new ideas from time to time.

Planning for a limited time, such as the five or six weeks of a teaching practice, involves consideration of the following:

1. The relationship of a particular topic to the course as a whole, the previous knowledge on which it is based and the topics to which it will lead.
2. The age, ability range and interests of the class concerned.
3. The amount of time needed for the introduction, development and consolidation of the work, and for testing.

This last entails breaking down the topic into lesson units, and it is helpful to first list the essential facts, but not necessarily in a teaching sequence at this stage. The first breakdown of work for a topic such as 'Respiration' may be:

a) Respiration is a process of energy release in living organisms.
b) It occurs in all living things. (Viruses being an exception—but is discussion relevant at this early stage?)
c) The energy produced is used in metabolic processes such as movement, synthesis and growth.
d) Enzymes located in mitochondria catalyse the process.
e) Glucose is the usual substrate.

f) Respiration may be aerobic or anaerobic.

g) ATP is an important energy transfer substance in cells.

It is now necessary to look at the work done previously by the class.
For example:

  (i)   Is this part of a topic on energy release in general?

  (ii) Have recent studies included any of the points listed above?

  (iii) Do the class understand the main concepts of photosynthesis?

  (iv) In what units do they measure energy? (S.I. units are not yet
        universally used.)

  (v)   How much work has been done on foods and feeding, food
        webs and ecology generally?

  (vi) Do the class yet distinguish between breathing and respiration?

An assessment of previous knowledge can be made by discussion
with the class teacher, or, in a new post, by examining work books and
questioning the class. It is not generally helpful to ask a class if they
have 'done' a topic. The normal answer is 10 per cent yes, 10 per cent
no and 80 per cent uncertain. Judicious questioning, such as 'How do
animals get energy?' 'For what do they use energy?' 'Do plants need
energy?' will enable one to judge the stage reached. Teachers leaving
a school should leave records of the work covered, and heads of
departments ought to know the stage reached by each class—but this
is not always so.

Colleges of Education usually suggest a format for the preparation
of schemes. These are designed to draw the attention of the students
to important considerations such as the age and ability of the class, the
length of lessons and the availability of laboratory space and equipment.
On these and similar considerations depends the exact type of teaching
to be done.

A completed scheme of work, derived from the list of respiration
points above may read:

Class III B

30 pupils, co-educational, average ability.

10 lessons of 1 hour 20 minutes, two per week.

Laboratory available for all lessons.

Topic: Respiration

Relevant previous knowledge:

Foods as an energy source. (S.I. units)
Photosynthesis.
Food webs (elementary knowledge).

Lesson outlines:

1. Respiration as a form of energy release. Circus of experiments and demonstrations, e.g. heat produced by cockroaches using differential air thermometer, movement in cockroaches, heat from germinating seeds.
2. Carbon dioxide production in respiration. Production by seeds, insects, earthworms, mammals, plant roots. Group practical work, different topic for each group. Results will be summarized and discussed with whole class.
3. Oxygen intake and rate of respiration. Group practical on oxygen consumption of small animals and seeds. CO_2 absorption for differences in volume (O_2 taken in and CO_2 given out). Short test.
4. Gas exchange in invertebrates, using Nuffield bicarbonate indicator. Specimens to include those for examination requirements. Group practical work.
5. The mechanism of breathing in a mammal. Model thorax and respiratory organs of sheep (fresh). Demonstration of functioning of lungs. Rate of breathing and activity.
6. Constituents of inhaled and exhaled air, using gas burettes. Group practical work. Short test.
7. Health hazards of smoking. Breathing and athletics training (from *Secondary Science* and *Nuffield Text III*). Demonstration 'smoking machine' and examination of products of combustion of tobacco.
8. Gas exchange in other vertebrates. Observation of fish and frog. Work cards to direct observation.
9. Anaerobic respiration in germinating seeds and yeast. Mitochondria and ATP in the living cell. Demonstration of muscle contraction with ATP.
10. Gas exchange in plans in light and dark, using bicarbonate indicator. Group practical work. Relate to photosynthesis. Test.

It is generally better, on a teaching practice, to give a number of short tests rather than one long examination at the end of the series of lessons. Short tests enable progress to be assessed so that lessons can be modified as necessary. This does not mean that the work rate is reduced to that of the slowest, or even the average pupil. The teacher must be a driving force in the classroom, and demand hard work, but he must be able to determine when his pupils are taken to the limit of their ability. Children respond best to work they feel is challenging, but still within their capabilities. There is always a minimum level of understanding which can be achieved by even the slowest learner, and there should be the opportunity for the more able to extend their work into more difficult areas.

Having worked out a scheme, it is necessary to plan each lesson in detail. It is unwise to plan more than one lesson ahead, as it is only to be expected that the scheme will be modified in the light of classroom experience. The most experienced teacher can prepare a lesson which proves to be a failure with a particular class. It is then necessary to repeat the work in a different way. Schemes of work frequently prove to be over-ambitious, though it is generally better to over-estimate rather than under-estimate the ability of a class.

2.3 Lesson notes

Lesson notes are made so as to clarify objectives and methods in the mind of the teacher. Adequate lesson notes are those which can be used by any biology teacher to give the lesson in the way intended by the person who prepared them.

Teachers and student teachers vary in the amount of detail they need to include in their notes. It is reasonable to expect the first notes of a first teaching practice to be very detailed, and then for them to become relatively brief. Much depends upon how much detail is needed by each student for a successful lesson.

It is important to realise that, just as a scheme of work is a forecast subject to continuous modification, lesson notes also are not a rigid framework. The exact procedure depends upon the response of a class to the introductory work, and on questions which arise. On the other hand, it is only by making a clear plan of a possible lesson sequence that a teacher can make use of the response of a class in attaining objectives of the lesson.

Essentials of a biology lesson

The main features of a typical biology lesson may be summarized as follows:

1. Whenever possible, living material from local habitats should be the basis of study.
2. Work should be presented as problem-solving situations. (Though it is unrealistic to expect pupils to 'discover' principles which are the result of many years work by eminent scientists! A sensible appraisal of what must be accepted and what can be discovered must usually be made by the teacher.)
3. A lesson generally must be based on previous knowledge.
4. Activities during the lesson must be varied.
5. Timing is important. In particular, there must be adequate time for discussion at the end of a lesson.
6. The work must be challenging, yet within the ability of the class.
7. Extra work should be available for the more able pupils.
8. Work should be consolidated by suitable homework.

Identifying the essential facts

For the second lesson in the respiration sequence suggested earlier it may be intended to use the Nuffield 'bicarbonate indicator' (*Nuffield 'Biology' Teachers' Guide III*, page 7). During the course of the lesson, pupils need to understand that:

  a) The indicator changes colour when acids are added.
  b) Carbon dioxide dissolves in water to give an acid solution.
  c) Burning glucose gives off carbon dioxide.
  d) Respiring tissues give off carbon dioxide. The giving off of carbon dioxide can be taken as an indication of the occurrence of respiration.

In what order are these facts best presented? How much detail of the working of the indicator is necessary at this stage? Confusion may result from discussing the use of the indicator in showing the removal of CO_2 as well as showing the increase in the amount of this gas.

It is reasonable to suppose that pupils are familiar with the use of litmus in chemistry lessons (this should, of course, be checked) and that the lime water test has been used. The idea of an indicator should not be new, and its use can be compared with litmus.

Once the working of the indicator has been explained and demonstrated, discussion leads to the design of experiments to find out which materials give off carbon dioxide. The production of the gas from burning glucose provides a useful basis for explaining the source of carbon dioxide in living tissue.

The need for control experiments must be clearly indicated. The resulting lesson note may be:

Class III B   Biology Laboratory
Date: 11-20 to 12-40
30 pupils

Topic   Respiration

Subject of lesson: The production of carbon dioxide during respiration by living tissues.

Materials and apparatus: 30 test tubes and stoppers, copper gauze or sponge platforms for tubes, hard glass tube fitted with delivery tube. Bicarbonate indicator. Cockroaches (or locusts), earthworms, guppies, germinating seeds, plant roots, potato tubers.
(Note: standard apparatus such as Bunsen burners and bench reagents such as lime water need not be indicated.)

Introduction: Reference to energy production by living organisms as seen in the last lesson. Compare burning glucose with respiration in that energy (heat) is evolved. Show production of CO_2 using lime water. (5−10 minutes)

Development:

1. Demonstrate the use of bicarbonate indicator using burning glucose and exhaled air. Show effect of tartaric acid on the indicator and the effect of CO_2 on litmus. (5 minutes)
2. Discuss how to test whether CO_2 is produced by the living organisms provided. Discuss the preparation of controls. (10 minutes)
3. Pupils work in groups of four, each using a different material. Results to be summarized on the blackboard, filling in a table prepared by the teacher. (30 minutes)

Material	Colour change in indicator	Time taken
5 g germinating seeds	red — yellow	6 min
5 g potato	red — yellow	15 min
5·4 g cockroaches (6)		

4. Enter the method (briefly) and the table for the full set of results in laboratory notebooks, whilst waiting for results.

Conclusion: Discussion of findings and summary of the important points.

Homework: Background reading from textbooks on gas exchange. (Give page reference and promise short test next lesson.)

It is helpful, during early stages of teaching, to prepare both the notes and diagrams which are to go on the blackboard, and an indication of the type of recording to be done in the pupils' laboratory notebooks.

Class notebooks

The chosen method depends very much on the ability of the class. It can be expected that a laboratory notebook will look as though it has been in the laboratory, though slovenly work should not be tolerated. It is useful to have a separate exercise book for background notes and homework, which will include examination-type questions.

Annotated diagrams to explain the arrangement of apparatus are a concise way of recording experimental methods. Such diagrams are also of use with slow learners (usually slow writers!) as the sole record of work done.

The experiment done in the lesson outlined above could be recorded as seen in Fig. 1 and followed by a summary of the results of the work of other groups and the conclusions to be drawn.

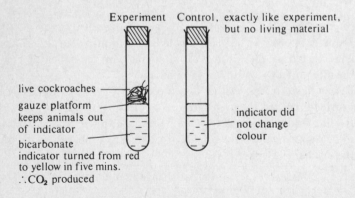

Fig. 1 To show whether cockroaches produce CO_2

Realistic educationists are aware that there are facts which must be recorded precisely by the whole class. Many teachers consider the only way to be sure of accuracy is to *give* notes, either by dictation, by providing duplicated copies or having their pupils copy notes from the blackboard. Certainly the notes thus obtained will be accurate, and they can be learnt parrot-fashion by the pupil. However, similar notes may be found in a textbook, but few teachers would expect their pupils to copy notes from a textbook into their exercise books. The value of a pupil's notebook is that the language and expressions used are easily understood by him—and the language he will most easily understand is that which he writes himself.

Teachers soon gain the ability to use expressions and a vocabulary suited to their classes. This ability is essential where the language of instruction is not the pupil's first language or where the standard of attainment in written language is low. In these cases copied notes can be useful, though understanding should be tested by setting written work in which the facts must be stated in the pupil's own words.

Alternatively, notes can be obtained from discussion with the class, written on the board by the teacher and subsequently copied into the pupils' notebooks. The disadvantage here is that many pupils make no contribution whatsoever. Generally, it is better to use a method in which each pupil must think about what he is writing. Recording and learning thus occur at the same time.

The following methods are arranged in order of difficulty. An average class, used to dictated notes, can be trained to write their own notes by progressing through the series.

1. *Giving incomplete notes with key words missing.*

'Carbon dioxide dissolves in water giving an . . . solution. The colour of the bicarbonate indicator is . . . at atmospheric concentrations of CO_2. When the proportion of CO_2 increases the indicator becomes a . . . colour'.

This method is especially suitable for junior classes, less able pupils at all levels, and pupils whose first language is not the language of instruction.

2. *Providing a series of questions to be answered.*

The answers to set questions form notes. It is necessary to train pupils to write complete sentences, and to frame questions so that the resulting notes 'flow'.

This method is relevant to average children at secondary level.

3. *Writing notes from a series of headings.*

Not generally applicable to junior classes, but of great value to senior pupils. Learning to read, experiment, discuss and then to write concise notes is a valuable asset and an important preparation for more advanced work. It may be argued that only the best pupils are able to make their own notes, but even if this is so, these able pupils must not be reduced to the level of achievement of the average. In fact, average pupils *can* be trained through the three stages to produce useful notes. Marking of these notes is a useful indication to the teacher of the level of understanding reached by the individual pupils.

Marking class notebooks

Opinions on the value of marking vary widely. Pupils need to be aware of their progress, and the fact that work is going to be assessed has a good effect on the amount of effort put in. Work therefore needs to be graded, and corrected. Putting corrections on workbooks is of doubtful value. Mistakes common to a number of pupils indicate the need for some remedial teaching, and therefore correction in class time.

Minor errors are better corrected by the pupil himself. All the teacher need do is draw attention to wrong statements and train pupils to ask for help whenever this is needed. It follows that teachers must ascertain that corrections have been done when the book is next in for marking.

The standard five point scale, with plus or minus signs, gives a reasonable indication of progress. Dividing a set of books into five piles on the basis of the standard of work is quick and reliable. Adjustments can be made as the books are checked over for errors of fact, spelling or punctuation. Wherever possible comments written on books should be encouraging. Work of very low standard should be discussed with individual pupils, and major common errors corrected with the whole class.

Consolidation of work

Facts and ideas presented once are not retained for long in the mind. It is necessary to give the same work in a different form in order to ensure understanding.

Ways of doing this include:

1. Setting background reading on the topic for homework. The *Nuffield Biology* texts provide relevant work of this type.

2. Application of knowledge in a new situation, usually by setting questions in which information is given and has to be explained using knowledge gained in the preceding lesson. Such a question relevant to the lesson discussed in detail above may be: Two tubes were set up containing in one, small pieces of potato tuber, and in the other an equal amount of plant roots. Bicarbonate indicator was added to cover the material, and the tubes stoppered. The indicator in the tube with roots changed to a yellow colour in 5 minutes, that in the tube with potato pieces changed in 30 minutes. What does this suggest about the rate of respiration of the two tissues? Suggest reasons for the different rates.

3. Setting standard examination questions. This has a dual purpose. Pupils are prepared for the type of question they will be expected to answer, and at the same time have to recall the subject matter of the previous lesson.

4. Setting short answer tests, for which pupils have been given home-work time, for reviewing specific areas of work. Checking and correcting such tests is as valuable in consolidating work as is the time spent in learning.

2.4 Work cards

Group work or individual work in class is facilitated by the provision of written instructions for observation or investigation. After a brief introduction and discussion of a topic, children can be set to work whilst the teacher is free to deal with individual problems. The amount of detail given may include background information as well as questions to be answered and suggestions for lines of approach. It is usually possible to include recording and even testing understanding. Such a 'work card' is given below.

Work card for testing starch content of leaves.

1. You are given two leaves; leaf A is from a plant which has been in continuous light for 12 hours and leaf B is from a plant which has been in darkness for 48 hours.

Grind leaf A with a little sand in the mortar, adding about 5 ml water. Tip the resulting mixture into a test tube, and boil for 2 minutes. Cool the tube under a running tap, and add a few drops of iodine solution. What do you notice?
What does this indicate about the materials present in the leaf?

Repeat the operation, using leaf B and *clean* apparatus.
What effect has the iodine on this leaf extract?
How can you explain the difference in the two leaves?

Complete the following notes in your laboratory notebooks:

The effect of light on green leaves.

Green leaves taken from a plant which has been exposed to light for 12 hours can be shown to contain . . . . This substance is formed during the process of . . . . Leaves which had been in darkness for 48 hours did not contain . . . . This suggests that light is necessary for . . . .

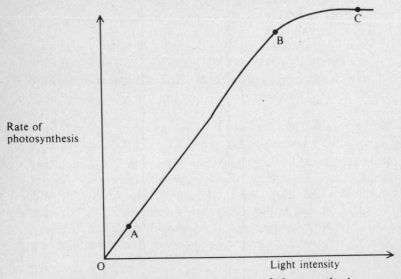

Fig. 2 Graph showing increase in rate of photosynthesis

2. The graph in Fig. 2 shows the rate of photosynthesis in a plant at different light intensities. (Do not copy the graph into your books.)
   How do you explain:
   a) The increase in the rate of photosynthesis between A and B?
   b) The shape of the curve between B and C?

2.5 Class organization

Demonstrations
   Demonstration of practical work is relevant when:

1. *A new technique is being shown.*
   When materials are small (e.g. inoculating bacterial cultures) it is necessary to demonstrate to groups rather than to a whole class.
   On other occasions, large scale apparatus can be used. The iodine test for starch is shown more clearly using a gas jar of starch solution than with a small test tube of reagents.

2. *Using elaborate apparatus which is in short supply.*
   This rarely happens in biology lessons. Usually such work can be incorporated in a 'circus'. Though certain apparatus such as kymographs and spectrometers are best set up by a teacher, pupils should be allowed to assist wherever possible.

3. *Using dangerous materials.*
   Pathogenic micro-organisms should not be used in schools, and there are certain regulations in Britain concerning the storage and use of radio-active substances. These latter are only used in Advanced level work. Much depends upon the age and laboratory experience of the class, where strong acids and alkalis are used. The gas absorption solutions used in respiration experiments described in the Nuffield Biology texts are highly caustic, and, if there is any chance of misuse by a class, should be handled by the teacher. If potentially explosive chemicals are used (in science lessons) a perspex safety screen is desirable.

4. *Introducing a new topic.*
   Demonstration experiments can be usefully employed to initiate discussion, especially if they are selected to give quick and impressive results.

5. *Apparatus of even the simplest kind is in short supply.*

Schools in many countries cannot yet afford the amount of apparatus required for group or individual work. In these cases, demonstration is infinitely more useful than mere theoretical learning, and it is possible to involve the class in the design and conducting of an experiment.

Group work

This is the most convenient way of carrying out class practical work. Discussion within a group if helpful, and progress is faster than in individual experimentation. It is easier for a teacher to circulate amongst eight or nine groups rather than try to discuss problems with thirty or more individuals.

Groups may be of mixed ability or graded within a class, though generally pupils work best with their friends. Teachers have to make sure that all members of a group participate, and none become too domineering or too passive. Group work involves movement and conversation, but there is an easily recognisable difference between a 'working' noise and undisciplined noise, which must be quelled. Providing that the work is within the ability of a class, discipline problems tend to be fewer than when teaching the class as a whole.

Where group work is new to a class, it is advisable to introduce it after a few lessons of classwork during which the new teacher is accepted by the class as the person firmly in charge of proceedings.

Individual work

Generally this involves observation of a specimen, microscope work or dissection. Observation should be guided by appropriate questioning, either orally or by work cards. A new specimen of living material has a special interest for the pupils, and a certain amount of time must be allowed for spontaneous observation. It is then necessary to draw attention to salient features and set a pattern of work to be followed.

A series of questions for a junior form observing a live fish may be:

How many fins can you see?
Are they in pairs or single?
Which seems to be the strongest fin?
Which fins move when the fish prepares to dive?
Do any of the fins 'fold up'? Which ones?
Why do you think the surface is smooth and slippery?

Such questions are not a rigid sequence, but a guide to significant observation.

Reading

Whether reading is set for homework or classwork (and there is no reason why some background reading should not form part of a 'circus' of work) it should be made meaningful by preparing a set of questions to be answered either verbally or in writing. Training in reading and notemaking is essential at an early stage of secondary school work.

Preparing apparatus

Ideally, every experiment carried out in class should have been tried out beforehand by the teacher. This is especially important during teaching practice, when topics are being taught for the first time. The responsibility for providing apparatus and materials is the teacher's, though the responsibility is usually delegated to a laboratory technician.

Many students are not fully aware of the problems faced by technicians who are working in more than one laboratory and for several teachers at the same time. It is unfair to expect apparatus to be provided at the last moment before a lesson. Several days' notice must be given, and the materials checked over by the teacher in sufficient time for mistakes to be rectified.

A laboratory must be left in a clean and tidy condition for the next occupants, and this is the responsibility of the teacher and pupils. Apparatus used needs to be collected and rinsed, especially if acids or caustic solutions have been used. Work places, including the teacher's demonstration bench, should be cleared and cleaned.

There are communities in certain countries where teachers and pupils consider it beneath their dignity to do any task which may be regarded as manual labour. Science teachers and their pupils must be prepared to maintain and set up their own apparatus and materials and to do their share in keeping laboratories in a tidy state. Failure to do so seems one of the most serious hindrances to progress in the sciences, particularly as in these communities technicians tend to have less training than in developed countries.

2.6 Examinations and tests

Examination methods are the subject of much current research, and there is extensive literature on all aspects of assessment. Only an outline of the main considerations can be given here.

Purpose of examinations

Tests and examinations enable:

1. An assessment of the attainment and skills of pupils.
2. Evaluation of the success of the teaching methods used.
3. Correction of faults and misconceptions.
4. The provision of a stimulus to learning.

What can be tested?

Any test questions must have clearly defined objectives. These may be:

1. Factual recall, in which knowledge of subject matter is assessed, without reference to the application of the facts, or to generalizations from them.
2. Practical skills.
3. Powers of observation.
4. Scientific thinking, where an experiment has to be designed to test a given hypothesis, or data has to be interpreted.
5. The ability to organize knowledge and express ideas in continuous prose, that is 'essay type' questions.

Setting examinations

An examination may include all aspects of testing mentioned above, or it may deal with specific aspects. Before an examination is prepared, it is essential to summarize the objectives of the course of work which is to be examined. This is true of terminal or yearly examinations, and of the type of examination given after several years' study. Once a list of objectives has been made, it is then possible to set the number and type of questions which relate to the defined objectives, and to their relative importance in the course of study.

Useful discussion of testing skills other than factual recall can be found in the *Schools Council Examinations Bulletin No. 8* [1].

public examination results. For example, if over the previous three years the biology grades in an external examination have been, on average, Grade 1 5 per cent, Grade 2 10 per cent, Grade 3 40 per cent, Grade 4 30 per cent, Grade 5 10 per cent and Grade 6 5 per cent, then it is reasonable to estimate that the top 5 per cent of this year's candidates will gain a Grade 1, 10 per cent a Grade 2 and so on.

Practical examinations

It should be obvious that these examinations test practical skills rather than theory—and that theory is used in interpretation of practical results. It is always difficult to persuade candidates that this *is* so, and poor grades in practical examinations are frequently the result of a conviction that a neatly drawn diagram, memorized from notes or a text, is more acceptable than a drawing of the observed features of the specimen concerned. Practical tests must therefore be set so that there is little chance of pure 'memory work' being produced by candidates.

The objectives of a practical examination can be summarized as the testing of:

1. Observation and inferences drawn from it.
2. Manipulative skill.
3. Design of experiments.

1 may be a demonstration experiment showing the original set up and the result, or an unfamiliar specimen to interpret.

2 may involve simple dissection or the carrying out of biochemical tests.
   (These two objectives may be tested by a single exercise, for example the testing of a food substance with reagents commonly used, and inferences made on the distribution of food within the specimen. e.g. Why is there an accumulation of protein at the root apex of mustard seed?)

3 will probably involve the provision of simple apparatus and materials, for example, tubes of Nuffield bicarbonate indicator and two respiring tissues, the candidate being required to find out which was respiring at the higher rate.

Up to O level, practical examinations have to be simple, because of the large numbers of candidates involved and the availability of apparatus and laboratory space. If it is impossible to set examinations which test the skills listed above, then it is better to assess practical work during routine term lessons. The provision of a specimen which has been used as a 'type' specimen in class to be 'drawn and labelled' is no real test of practical skill.

Bibliography

1. The Certificate of Secondary Education: Experimental Examinations: Science Examinations Bulletin No. 8. The Schools Council. London H.M.S.O. 1965.
2. The Certificate of Secondary Education: An introduction to objective-type examinations. Examinations Bulletin No. 4. Secondary Schools Examinations Council. London. H.M.S.O. 1964.
3. The Certificate of Secondary Education: An introduction to some techniques of examining. Examinations Bulletin No. 3. Secondary Schools Examinations Council. London. H.M.S.O. 1964.

Note: These bulletins are equally useful for teachers in schools taking G.C.E. examinations.

See also:

Bremner, J.   Teaching Biology. Macmillan 1967

Head, J.J.   New Questions in O level Biology. Oliver & Boyd 1967
   Book 1   The Mammal
   Book 2   Plants and Invertebrates
   Book 3   Genetics
   Book 1   Teachers' Guide
   Book 2   Teachers' Guide
   Book 3   Teachers' Guide

Nuffield Secondary Science. Examining at C.S.E. Level. Longman 1971

LABORATORIES AND EQUIPMENT

3.1 Laboratory planning

Work space

The essential requirements for a biology teaching laboratory are few. A space in which to work, a good source of light, a water supply and a flexible arrangement of tables and chairs are all that are required. Many other fixtures and fittings are desirable, but, given this minimum, biology can be successfully taught to O level Certificate of Education. Electricity supplies and a gas supply (mains or bottled gas) are not essential. There are many countries in which the majority of secondary schools have neither. Spirit lamps are an adequate source of heat for work in biology, and charts and photographs take the place of projected visual aids.

No two teachers will agree on the exact design of an ideal laboratory. Fig. 3 is a simple general plan developed for schools having only limited funds. It illustrates the main features on which more elaborate plans can be developed if funds are available. In the developed countries plans for laboratories and ancillary areas are available from the Inspectorate and Science Teachers' Associations. Local authorities frequently have a standard design for school science blocks, adapted to suit local needs.

$3m^2$ per pupil is regarded as a suitable area to allow, on the assumption that classes will consist of 30 pupils. Advanced laboratories for small groups need a slightly larger space per pupil, but many schools have to make do with much more crowded conditions.

Aspect

Assuming the laboratory is on the ground floor for easy access to outdoor areas, consideration should be given to the amount of light reaching various areas. In cool climates in the northern hemisphere one long wall of the laboratory facing north gives suitable conditions for aquaria. The opposite south-facing wall will be suitable for plant growth and the siting of a greenhouse or Wardian screen (an extended window, enclosed in glass on all sides, thus functioning as a greenhouse).

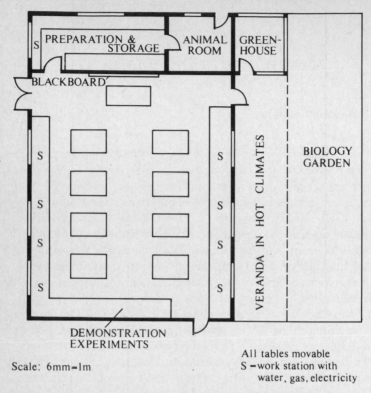

Scale: 6mm=1m

All tables movable
S —work station with
    water, gas, electricity

Aspect depends upon geographical position and climate

Fig. 3 Simple plan for a biology laboratory

In hot climates, extended eaves are necessary to shade windows, and in some areas it is advisable to have a blank wall (or one having high level windows) facing the prevailing sunlight.

Ancillary areas

Preparation rooms ideally have access from both inside and outside the laboratory. Each should have a hot and cold water supply, and some means of heating and weighing substances. Preparation rooms often double as storerooms, though it is as well to provide a separate room for bulk stores of chemicals and glassware, as well as textbook storage.

An animal room, not communicating with the laboratory, is useful to keep small mammals, aquaria, insect breeding cages and cultures which may be contaminated by fumes or damaged by unauthorized investigation in the laboratory. In hot climates, an outside shelter serves the same purpose. A covered way from the laboratory and preparation room is necessary for the rainy season.

In cool climates, a greenhouse or a Wardian case is essential for growing plants. In the tropics a veranda outside the laboratory, with easy access to a water supply, enables pot plants to be grown, while protected from natural hazards such as drying out, insect pests and grazing animals.

Safety

Local authorities in the United Kingdom have certain bye-laws concerning safety in laboratories. Even where no such restrictions apply, certain precautions need to be taken to prevent accidents.

1. At least one fire blanket and chemical fire extinguisher should be provided, and pupils should know how to use them.
2. Doors should open outwards in case of explosion, and no room, including ancillary rooms, should have only one exit.
3. Electricity supplies to apparatus should be low voltage. If low voltage is not available, microscopes should have a separate lamp for illumination, rather than a built in one. Projectors normally have built in transformers.

   If power supply sources are fitted to benches, they must be a good distance from water taps, so that it is not possible to reach both at the same time.
4. Poisons should be clearly labelled as such, and locked away when not in use.
5. Highly inflammable liquids should be labelled, and not used near a flame or in electrical apparatus such as drying ovens and centrifuges.
6. A first aid kit should be readily available.
7. In countries where alcohol is dutiable, supplies have to be locked away and consumption recorded. Customs officials have the right to demand to inspect record books and storage.

Furniture and fittings

Modern laboratories have fixed side benches with water, gas and electricity supplies grouped as work stations. Movable tables and chairs occupy the rest of the room, and can be grouped according to the type of lesson in progress.

As some time is spent sitting at microscopes, the tables in a biology laboratory are generally lower than those in other laboratories. However, the main consideration is that the heights of the table and chairs correspond so that there is leg and knee room. With the increasing use of laboratories for combined sciences, and the reduction in the amount of detailed histology in biology courses, the standard 3 foot table and bench is preferable, with chairs or stools rather higher than usual. Allow a 9 inch space as a minimum between seat and table. Movable tables can be fitted with plugs for bench lights, and the table circuit connected by a cable to the supply to the fixed side benches, when necessary.

Individual work stations should have water, gas and electricity supplies. There also needs to be one large sink with a high swan neck tap for washing burettes and similar apparatus. All sinks must have a trap for the inevitable debris.

Adequate cupboards and display cases, some lockable, must be provided in laboratory and preparation rooms. Bulletin boards can occupy any spare wall space, and a blackboard should be sited so that it is shaded from direct sunlight. Demonstration benches are used less frequently nowadays, and a fixed bench at the front of the room is not recommended.

Lighting

The laboratory should be well lit, and special lighting is needed for:

1. *Microscopes*—standard microscope lamps with 40 watt bulbs are adequate for elementary work. In the tropics, daylight is sufficient for most microscope work (not oil immersion magnifications), and is less trying than artificial sources.
2. *Plants*—potted plants, alga cultures and photosynthesis experiments are aided by the provision of special fluorescent (cold) light, which can be left on 24 hours a day. Twin tubes mounted 3 feet above a concrete or formica topped bench are all that is necessary, though the area can be enclosed by a glass fronted screen, adequately ventilated.

Blackout

Many modern 'daylight' screens do not require a full blackout of the laboratory, though micro-projectors and film projectors do not give good results, whatever the manufacturer's claims. A good black-out arrangement is therefore necessary if much work with projected materials is done. In hot climates an extractor fan will be needed, as any form of blackout reduces ventilation.

Working surfaces

Wood is the cheapest and best wearing surface in most countries. It can be kept in good condition by the regular application of linseed oil. Plastic surfaces are becoming more popular. The good quality plastics resist acids and most organic solvents.

Flooring

Acid-proof plastics, either as tiles or self-hardening liquids, are suitable. In warm climates cement or concrete is cheap and easy to maintain.

Wastes

The end products of dissections, micro-organism cultures and the like, become both unpleasant and a health hazard if not disposed of as soon as possible. Bacterial cultures must be sterilized before disposal. Sink waste disposal units are ideal for a biology laboratory. Otherwise, wastes should be incinerated, or buried in a pit which is regularly burnt-out—this latter should be the rule in hot countries where there is no convenient boiler house fire.

3.2 Apparatus

The purchase of apparatus is normally controlled by a strict annual budget, within which Heads of Departments are free to choose the most suitable supplies for the courses taught in their subject. Scientific supply agencies provide standard lists of basic equipment, and special lists for certain courses such as the Nuffield sciences. These lists need to be treated with caution. It is certainly not essential to purchase every item in the quantities suggested, and schools on limited budgets will find themselves able to manage with much less. However, none of the lists from the main suppliers can be regarded as extravagant, and teachers faced with equipping a new laboratory will find a supplier's catalogue a most helpful basis on which to work.

Standard apparatus

Glass apparatus is often replaced nowadays with plastic ware. Some plastics are not resistant to strong acids and alkalis, nor to certain organic solvents. Their properties are usually stated in the supplier's catalogue. For work not involving heating, or corrosive chemicals, plastic apparatus proves cheaper, much more durable than glass, and as easy to clean. The accuracy of, for example, measuring cylinders, is not as good as the glass model, but is usually adequate for elementary work.

Balances

Chemical balances involve time-consuming weighing processes, and one automatic balance can be bought for the same cost as the larger number of chemical balances required for class use. It is therefore recommended that one automatic balance and one Butchart or similar balance are all that is required in a school biology laboratory. A few spring balances and a depression balance are required for some experimental work in Nuffield Biology courses. Chemical balances and automatic models must be kept on a firm bench of stone or concrete.

Heating

The standard Bunsen burner, and its modified form for butane gas, is the most convenient form of heating. Butane gas may be from mains or cylinder sources. Electric hot plates reduce fire risks from inflammable liquids, and laboratory types are being designed in greater variety.

Where gas and electricity supplies do not exist, spirit burners are adequate for most biology work, and in some areas in rural parts of the tropics kerosene stoves are used—but this should be avoided where possible because of the high risk of fire.

Electrical apparatus

It is necessary to state the local supply voltage when ordering any electrical equipment, and spares such as lamps should be ordered at the same time. Where electricity supplies are unreliable, mechanical apparatus (e.g. a clinostat working by a clock mechanism) is preferable.

Microscopes

Many excellent and inexpensive microscopes are available for elementary work. As microscopes represent the greatest capital outlay for a single item of equipment, they must be chosen with care. For elementary work the number required is not great, and one monocular microscope to four pupils should be adequate. Thus, if the average class is 40 pupils, 10 microscopes are needed. One demonstration microscope, with an oil immersion lens, and several binocular microscopes and/or dissection lenses are needed in addition to the monoculars.

Schools on limited budgets need to consider the merits of using 2 X 2″ colour slides in place of individual microscope slides. In relation to the cost of equipment, the small experience of microscopy obtained in elementary courses is insignificant.

Ordering supplies

Equipment is usually classed as consumable or capital (non-consumable) items. The former includes chemicals, test tubes, filter papers and similar items which have to be constantly replaced. An annual allowance is normally made for such items. Capital equipment is rarely replaced, being microscopes, projectors, balances and the like. An allowance for these is made from time to time when a new laboratory has to be equipped or when the number of pupils increases or the type of course is changed.

Consumables and non-consumables are ordered from supply agencies, and any of those advertizing regularly in the School Science Review will be found to be reliable. They all have agencies in overseas countries, who deal with importation of orders and keep local supplies of standard items.

Some local authorities in the U.K. appoint an agent for all their science supplies. Where a teacher has to choose between suppliers, experience will show which are the most reliable and prompt in dealing with orders.

Biology teachers need to have a small amount of petty cash for the purchase of fresh material, seeds, fruits, animal food etc. A careful record of purchases should be kept, and bills obtained.

Stock book

All equipment, consumable and non-consumable, should be recorded on arrival and checked at least once a year. Often the stock-taking can be done by the laboratory technician, though the teacher in charge is ultimately responsible. A convenient arrangement shows the stock at the start of the school year, the stock at the end of the year, and the amount consumed during the year. This is useful in estimating future purchases.

Capital items generally have a serial number stamped on a metal part of the apparatus. This is conveniently recorded in the stock book, and will be needed in case of theft for identification purposes, and when the apparatus is sent for servicing.

Breakages

Many schools insist that pupils pay for any apparatus which they break, whether the breakage was due to carelessness or a pure accident. A record of breakages must therefore be kept, and is also useful in estimating replacement purchases.

Maintenance of apparatus

Microscopes, projectors, electric ovens, centrifuges need to be regularly overhauled by the manufacturer or his agent. In the United Kingdom the main supply firms send staff round schools to inspect and service equipment which they have supplied. All apparatus lasts longer and works more efficiently if it is regularly inspected by the teacher or laboratory technician. Apparatus with moving parts should be regularly cleaned and oiled (though the rack and pinion of microscopes should *not* be oiled). Lenses should be cleaned with lens paper every time the instrument is used, and the mirror and stage kept dust free. Projector lenses need as much care as microscope lenses.

Glass and plastic ware is best cleaned by any standard liquid detergent. It may be cheaper to buy bulk supplies from a science supply firm, though nowadays local supermarkets can be a better source of supply, no delivery charges being involved.

Storage

Some teachers prefer to make sets of apparatus which are kept in cupboards at pupil's work stations in the laboratory. Others find central storage more convenient, and this method is necessary when supplies are limited. It is also easier to check breakages and cleanliness, and to take stock.

Special apparatus

The following items are not essential, but, if they can be afforded, simplify many laboratory processes.

1. *Refrigerator*
Uses:
 (i) Storage of specimens for a series of dissections. Refrigeration is preferable to preservation in formalin after the first dissection session.
 (ii) Storage of certain reagents, for example ATP.

2. *Centrifuge*
Uses:
 (i) Concentrating cultures of aquatic micro-organisms.
 (ii) Anaesthetizing ciliates and flagellates. Mild centrifugation is said to distort the cytoplasm enough to render an organism immobile.
Hand centrifuges are quite adequate for school work.

3. *Thermostatically controlled oven*
Uses:
 (i) Incubating bacterial and mould cultures.
 (ii) Drying materials for dry weight or water content estimates. (e.g. soil samples.)
 (iii) Incubation of Drosophila.
 (iv) Incubation of chick eggs—the oven must be very well ventilated and humidified.

4. *Thermostatically controlled water baths*
Uses:
 (i) Enzyme reaction experiments.
 (ii) Preparing nutrient agar media, prior to sterilization.
 (iii) Extraction of chlorophyll with ethanol. The risk of fire is much less than with a naked flame.

5. *Electric blender*
Uses:
 (i) For pulping tissues prior to separation in the centrifuge.
 (ii) For making up solutions which require constant stirring *provided* these will not corrode the material of which the blender is made.

6. *Pressure cooker or autoclave*

Uses: Sterilizing apparatus and media for micro-organism cultures.

A domestic pressure cooker is sufficient for school work, and much less costly than a similar capacity autoclave.

7. *De-ioniser*

Use: Provides a supply of pure water through the apparatus from mains supply. Distilled water can usually be obtained from the chemistry department's still—but a ready supply 'on tap' in the biology laboratory is useful. The amount needed does not justify purchase of a still just for the biology department. De-ionisers are only economical where the cartridges can be exchanged locally.

3.3 Standard reagents and their uses

Percentage solutions

These solutions are not intended to be made up with extreme accuracy. It is sufficient for, say a 10% solution, to add 10 g of the solute to 90 ml of the solvent.

Normal solutions

A normal solution contains 1 g equivalent of the solute in 1 litre of solution. Bench acids are N/10 solutions, and can be made from the concentrated solutions to the degree of accuracy required for elementary work by assuming that:

Concentrated sulphuric acid is approximately 36N

Concentrated hydrochloric acid is approximately 11N

Concentrated nitric acid is approximately 10N

Remember to add acids to water and not water to acids as there is considerable heat generated by the formation of the solution.

Reagents, stains, enzymes and indicators

Acetocarmine

Use: Chromosome staining. Aceto-orcein or Feulgen give better results, but carmine is more readily obtainable in certain countries.

Preparation: Reflux 5 g (excess) carmine with 45 ml water and 55 ml glacial acetic acid. If a reflux condenser is not available, simmer the mixture in a conical flask in a fume cupboard. Filter before use.

Aceto-orcein

Use: Chromosome staining.

Preparation: Exactly as for acetocarmine, but substituting 5 g orcein for the carmine. Proprionic acid can be used in place of acetic, and some authorities consider the results to be better.

Acetic-alcohol fixative

Use: Precipitates chromatin, therefore used to fix tissues before chromosome staining.

Preparation: 1 part by vol. glacial acetic acid to 3 parts ethyl alcohol (or Industrial Methylated Spirits if available). Material should be fixed for at least an hour, and preferable longer. It will keep indefinitely in this fixative at low temperatures, and up to two weeks at temperatures above 25°C.

Alcohols

Use: In fixatives, as a preservative, for dehydration in preparing microscopic material, as a solvent for chlorophyll and in the preparation of certain reagents. Ethyl alcohol is the most generally useful. It can be bought very cheaply in the United Kingdom as 'Industrial Methylated Spirit', approximately 95% ethyl alcohol, the remainder being methyl alcohol and water. A permit is required for its use, and is easily obtained by educational establishments. Asbolute alcohol is expensive and not necessary for elementary work. As alcohol is obtainable duty free for school use, a record has to be kept of stock and amounts used, and undiluted stock has to be locked away. Customs officials have the right to inspect storage and record books.

Preparation: A mixture of alcohol and water undergoes a shrinkage in volume. For fixatives and preservatives, there is no need to dilute with great accuracy. A 30% alcohol solution as a general preservative is merely 30ml alcohol plus 70ml water.

Agar

Use: As a setting agent for culture of bacteria and fungi, as it is not affected by the enzymes they produce. These are often proteolytic, therefore gelatine is not always suitable as a setting agent.

Preparation: 1 g agar dissolved in 100 cm^3 water at 70/80°C. Nutrients and salts are added as required for the culture of specific organisms, and the medium is sterilized before use at 15 lbs pressure for 20 minutes (or 7 kg for 20 minutes). At high ambient temperatures, 1·2 to 1·5 g agar per 100 cm^3 water is needed, and in high humidity petri dishes of the medium are best stored in a desiccator if air-conditioning is not available.

Barium sulphate
Use: Precipitation of soil colloids when testing for pH.
Preparation: Use dry, in equal quantities with soil.

Benedict's reagent
Use: Qualitative and quantitative testing of reducing sugars. It is superior to Fehling's solutions as it is non-caustic, keeps well, and can be used quantitatively.
Preparation: Ready prepared, or:
  17·3 g copper sulphate crystals
  173 g sodium citrate
  100 g sodium carbonate
Dissolve all reagents in water and make up to 1 litre.

Bicarbonate indicator (Nuffield)
Use: Shows the increase or decrease in carbon dioxide. It is a mixture of Thymol Blue, Cresol Red and sodium bicarbonate. The latter roughly doubles the pH shift caused by changes in CO_2 concentration.

The indicator is brought to equilibrium with atmospheric air immediately before use. The colour then appears orange-red in a test tube, deeper red in larger quantities. As the CO_2 concentration decreases, the colour changes to purple. As the amount of CO_2 increases the indicator becomes yellow.

The reaction depends upon the fact that CO_2 forms an acid solution in water. Strong acids cause a further colour shift at about pH 1·8, and therefore should not be used to show colour changes. Tartaric acid, a weak acid, is suitable to demonstrate the colour changes to a class prior to use of the indicator.

The indicator can be brought to equilibrium with atmospheric air by bubbling air through the indicator in a filter flask. If Buchner filters are not available, small quantities of the indicator can be brought to equilibrium by bubbling air through by means of a dropping pipette, or in larger quantities, a hand bellows or a bicycle pump. This should be done with the same air as used in the control, that is laboratory air.

Preparation: 0·2 g Thymol Blue
                0·1 g Cresol Red

Dissolve these in 20 ml ethanol. Dissolve 0·84 g Analar sodium bicarbonate in 900 ml distilled water. Mix the two solutions, and dilute 10X for laboratory use.

Buffer solutions
Use: Occasionally used in elementary work for the growth of certain bacteria. Best obtained as buffer solution tablets from main suppliers, various pH ranges being obtainable.

Canada balsam
Use: A resin solution for permanent microscope preparations. It yellows with age, and euparal is better (see below).

Calcium chloride
Use: As a dehydrating agent, though it is not so efficient as silica gel (q.v.). Can be used to establish humidity gradients in response experiments. A self-indicating mixture of calcium chloride (with a small amount of cobalt chloride) is best for general use.

Cellosolve
Use: Dehydration of tissues for microscope preparations. Wet material can be put straight into the liquid, and it is preferable to a series of alcohols for the small amount of permanent preparations made in elementary courses. Stains such as Safranin/Light Green and Haematoxylin/Eosin can be obtained made up in cellosolve.

Cobalt chloride paper
Use: Detection of water, the colour changing from blue (dry) to pink when wetted.
Preparation: Dip filter paper in a 5% aqueous solution, of cobalt chloride, and allow to dry in a warm oven. Store in a desiccator, or in a jar with silica gel.

Culture solutions
see 'Knop's Solution' and 'Mineral Deficiency Solutions.'

Dichlorphenol indophenol
Use: Estimating Vitamin C content.
Preparation: Make up a 0·1% solution in water, and titrate against a standard solution of ascorbic acid, using a hypodermic syringe for measuring the volume. Compare with the volume of DCPIP which will just remain blue in various citrus fruit and vegetable juices.

Enzymes
Enzymes are available as solids, or as solutions. A useful proteolytic enzyme which keeps well is pepsin in glycerine, obtainable from chemists. Pepsin tablets from the same source also keep well. For experimental purposes solid enzymes are generally made up as 5% solutions.

Eosin
Use: Showing the path of water conduction in vascular plants, or as a counter-stain for animal tissues stained with haematoxylin.
Preparation: For showing xylem tissue, make up a 5% aqueous solution by first dissolving 5 g in alcohol (about 10 ml) and adding water to 100 ml total volume. As a microscopic stain eosin is usually prepared as a 1% solution in alcohol.

Euparal
A clear resin for mounting permanent microscope slides. It is best obtained ready prepared.

Fehling's solutions
Use: Testing qualitatively for reducing sugars. Benedict's reagent is preferable.

Solution A
69·3 g copper sulphate
1 litre distilled water

Solution B
250 g potassium hydroxide
346 g sodium potassium tartrate
1 litre distilled water
The solution should be stored in dark bottles. Add a few drops of solution A to the substrate under test. Add solution B until there is a deep blue colour. On heating, a yellow, orange or red precipitate indicates the presence of a reducing sugar.

Feulgen stain
Use: Chromosome staining. Best bought ready made up.

Formalin
Use: As a general preservative.
Preparation: Make up the strength of solution required from the 40% solution usually supplied. A 5% solution is most satisfactory.

Gelatine
Use: For bacteria culture media when agar is not obtainable. The proteolytic enzymes secreted by many bacteria will liquify gelatine media.
Preparation: 5g per 100ml water sets at temperatures up to 25°C. Higher ambient temperatures require a larger quantity of gelatine.

Glycerol
Use: For temporary microscope preparations. Glycerol has the same refractive index as air, and being hygroscopic, it does not dry out.
Preparation: Undiluted or as a 5% solution. The solution should have an antibacterial preparation added to it. If a standard preparation is not available, a very small amount of phenol can be added.

Haematoxylin
Use: Stain for animal tissues, with an eosin counter-stain.
Preparation: Best bought ready made up.

Indicators
In addition to the bicarbonate indicator mentioned above, indicators are needed in elementary fieldwork to estimate pH values of soil and water. Universal indicator, as liquid or as test papers, is sufficient. Narrow range indicator papers can be bought for more precise work. Generally the range encountered is from pH5 to pH8.

Indigo-carmine
Use: A useful redox indicator for testing the evolution of oxygen from submerged plants. A 5% solution is just decolourized with sodium dithionite solution (q.v.). Oxygen in small quantities restores the blue colour.

Indolacetic acid (IAA)
Use: Plant growth experiments.

Preparation: Can be obtained as a 1% lanolin paste, suitable for school experiments.

Iodine
Use: Forms a blue-black starch/iodine compound when added to starch. The compound is unstable to heat.

Preparation: An aqueous solution is used for starch testing. Iodine is insoluble in water, but soluble in a 1% potassium iodide solution. Grind 10 g iodine with 10 g potassium iodide, adding distilled water whilst grinding continues. Make up the resulting solution to 1 litre. To use, dilute the solution to a pale brown colour. Otherwise the test colour is masked. Alcohol solutions are not suitable for starch testing as ethanol affects the formation of the coloured starch/iodine compound.

Janus Green B (Diazine green)
Use: As a vital stain (non-toxic) for living material and a redox indicator. A clear blue aqueous solution turns pink under anaerobic conditions— for example in a yeast suspension. The colour change is much more rapid than the decolourization of methylene blue.

Preparation: As a 1% solution, in water.

Knop's solution
Use: A culture solution for plants, either supplied to the roots or for aquatic plants, including algae.

Preparation: Can be bought as tablets containing the necessary substances in the correct proportions.

>   Magnesium sulphate 0·1 g
>   Potassium hydrogen phosphate 0·2 g
>   Potassium nitrate 1·0 g
>   Calcium nitrate 0·1 g

All dissolved in 250 ml distilled water, adding the calcium salt last to prevent precipitation. Add 3 drops of ferric chloride as a 4% solution.

Lactophenol Blue
Use: Stain for fungi and nematodes.

Preparation: Best bought ready made up, together with lactophenol for washing the stained material.

Lime water
Use: Testing for carbon dioxide.

Preparation: Keep a Winchester of water with excess calcium hydroxide. Shake occasionally, and filter as required, topping up the Winchester with distilled water.

Mercuric chloride
Use: A 0·1% solution sprayed or painted over herbarium specimens prevents them being attacked by moulds. This is only necessary in tropical regions. *The salt is poisonous to humans.*

Mercury
Use: In manometers and for transpiration experiments. Also for making Millon's reagent. Mercury is a cumulative poison, which can be absorbed through the skin and inhaled as a vapour. It should therefore be used and stored with care.

Methylene Blue
Use: As a vital stain and as a redox indicator.
Preparation: As a 1% aqueous solution. When used for staining fungi a little detergent should be added as a wetting agent.

Methyl cellulose
Use: Slowing down protozoa for microscopic examination.
Preparation: As a 4% solution in water.

Millon's reagent
Use: Testing for proteins.
Preparation: 1 ml mercury dissolved in 20 ml c. nitric acid in a fume cupboard, and then diluted by *adding the mixture* to 50 ml water. Extreme care must be taken not to inhale the fumes. A better method, using mercuric sulphate, is described in *Nuffield Biology Teachers' Guide III*, p. 68. The reagent is really best obtained ready made up.

Neutral Red
Use: As a vital stain, especially for protozoans and rotifers.
Preparation: Make up a 5% aqueous solution.

Phenyl thiourea (PTC, Phenyl thiocarbamide)
This substance has recently been shown to be poisonous to small mammals. Until more definite information is available, it is not advisable to use the substance in schools. Originally it was used in genetics teaching, as the ability to taste the compound is inherited in a Mendelian way.

Phloroglucinol
Use: Staining lignin in plant tissues, in thin sections or on the surface of larger structures, e.g. one year old twigs cut transversely.
Preparation: Dissolve 5 g phloroglucinol in 10 ml alcohol, and make up to 250 ml with distilled water. Soak the tissue in the stain for 2—3 minutes, and add concentrated hydrochloric acid. A bright red colour develops in lignified tissues.

Potassium hydroxide
Use: The absorption of carbon dioxide in respiration experiments.
Preparation:
(i) As a 50% solution, add 50 g pellets to 50 ml water, a few at a time cooling and stirring constantly. A mechanical stirrer is advisable. There is a good deal of heat produced, and unless the mixture is stirred the pellets stick to the glass of the container.
(ii) Filter paper soaked in the above solution can be used in place of the liquid in apparatus of small volume e.g. in test tubes and ignition tubes when testing the rate of oxygen intake in respiration experiments.

Pyrogallol
Use: Absorption of oxygen in respiration experiments.
Preparation: Place 20 g resublimed pyrogallol in a 500 ml reagent bottle. Add 200 ml saturated potassium hydroxide solution (prepared as above) and, quickly, about 50 ml liquid paraffin. This makes an upper layer which excludes oxygen. Swirl the bottle until the pyrogallol is dissolved. Remove the solution as required with a glass pipette or large hypodermic syringe. For the preparation and storage of large quantities see *Nuffield Biology Teachers' Guide III*, p. 17—18.

Resazurin
Use: Testing the bacterial content of milk. It gives a quicker reaction than methylene blue, though this can be used if resazurin is not obtainable.
Preparation: Bought in tablet form. The colour changes from blue to pink to white in the presence of coliform and lactic acid bacteria. Protect the mixtures from strong light, which also affects the indicator.

Ringer solution
Use: Keeping fresh material in a solution isotonic with body fluids of the animal concerned.

Preparation: As tablets from most supply agencies (specify 'Mammalian Ringer'). Mammalian Ringer consists of 9g sodium chloride, 0·4g potassium chloride, 0·24g anhydrous calcium chloride and 0·2g sodium bicarbonate dissolved in 1 litre of distilled water.

Sodium dithionite
Use: To decolourize Indigo Carmine in oxygen production experiments.
Preparation: Make up a 1% solution, in a fume cupboard.

Soda lime
Use: Absorbs carbon dioxide when damp. It is a mixture of caustic soda and calcium hydroxide.

Sodium hydroxide
Use: Can be used in place of potassium hydroxide q.v.

Starch solution
Use: As a substrate for enzyme reactions.
Preparation: Mix 1g starch with 10ml water. Boil 90ml water in a 250ml beaker. As it comes to the boil add the starch and water mixture and stir to avoid frothing over. Boil for half a minute, and cool the solution before use.

Sudan III
Use: As a stain for fats and oils. It cannot be washed out of these substances, whereas it is readily washed out of non-fatty substances.
Preparation: Best bought ready prepared.

Silica gel
Use: A dehydrating agent for desiccators and for establishing humidity gradients in response experiments. The self-indicating kind, mixed with cobalt chloride, is advisable. The gel can be dried out in a warm oven.

Xylol
Use: A clearing agent in microscopy. It makes tissues translucent, and is miscible with Canada Balsam and Euparal.

3.4 Visual and Audio-visual aids

USES

These teaching aids range from the blackboard to modern inventions such as videotape. Before investing in expensive equipment, it is necessary to consider the value of items in the teaching of a course in a particular school.

Aids are used to explain difficult concepts, or to illustrate processes which cannot be shown in any other way—for example, industrial processes, or growth, or cell division condensed by time-lapse photography.

Difficult concepts in biology

The biological concepts generally needing teaching aids are:

1. *Three-dimensional structures*

Relating transverse and longitudinal sections to three dimensional structures involves great difficulty at early stages. Stem and leaf structure, and animal structures such as villi and kidney tubules are commonly discussed in elementary work. Their three dimensional structure can be demonstrated by:

  (i) Stereoscopic diagrams. These are not always easy to follow as they do not dispose of the difficulty of imagining three dimensions from a plane drawing.

 (ii) Commercially produced models. Many of these are excellent, but expensive.

(iii) Models made in school. Though simple, these are frequently the most effective, especially if made by the pupils themselves. A plasticine model of a stem, built up from a cylinder of one colour (the medulla), surrounded by 'vascular bundles' of a different colour, and in turn covered by a cortex, can then be cut into transverse, and longitudinal sections, and related to a specimen of a living stem. The latter is important. Models are not a replacement for the actual structure, but a means of understanding them.

Stem root and leaf structure as seen in transverse and longitudinal sections can be drawn on the sides of a box, or, more permanently, painted on the sides of a cube. Science Club members can often help in the preparation of simple models of this type.

2. *Time*

  (i) Geological Time. Analogy with a familiar time scale can help, though the appreciation of the vast time involved is a most difficult concept at any stage. A commonly used analogy is the comparison of the development of our planet and the life upon it with a 24 hour clock, on which scale man would appear on the scene only a few seconds before the end of the 'day'. An evolutionary wall chart, built up gradually with pictures and models of the organisms appearing at each stage, can also be helpful.

(ii) Time for growth and development. Direct experience is not always possible. Processes such as cell division are often shown by time-lapse filming, with no clear idea of the actual time involved being given. The idea of such processes as being continuous and taking a certain average time must be clearly explained.

3. *Size*

Magnifying aids are all too often used without making clear the relationship between the actual and the observed size of the specimen. The simplest means of estimating the size of objects viewed with a monocular microscope is by direct comparison with a familiar object or unit of macroscopic size. A transparent ruler, marked in millimeters, or two ink lines 1 mm apart on translucent paper can be viewed with high and low power lenses. A rough estimate of the extent of each field of view should be made, and the idea of the micron introduced as a necessary subdivision of the millimeter.

The more able pupils will be able to estimate the size of objects viewed as a proportion of the diameter of the field. Others will at least have gained an idea of the range of size involved. At advanced level it is necessary to measure accurately using an eyepiece graticule and stage micrometer, and to relate the drawings made to the actual size by stating the magnification. (The magnification of the drawing should not be confused with the magnification of the lens system used!) At any level the actual size of the specimen should be stated with any diagrams made.

The approximate magnification of a lens system is the product of the ocular and the objective magnification. Thus a 10X eyepiece and a 10X objective gives a 100X magnification. If an object just fills the low power (X100) field its diameter is approximately 1 400 microns (1·4mm). A drawing of this object measuring 7cm diameter represents a magnification of 50X (size of drawing divided by size of object).

AUDIO-VISUAL APPARATUS

1. *Micro-projectors*

Uses: Projecting an image formed by a microscope so that is is large enough to be seen by a group. The features to be observed can be pointed out; and where slides or material are in short supply, viewing a projected image can replace individual microscope work.

Types:

(i) A projection head incorporating a daylight screen, and an illuminating system for the adaptation of any monocular microscope.

(ii) A specialist projector, not usable as an ordinary microscope, with a system of interchangeable lenses, slide holders and tanks for live material. There should be a mirror to enable horizontal or vertical projection, and a cooling tank to place between lamp and live tanks. Iodine-quartz lamp illumination gives the most brilliant image.

Care and maintenance: As with other projection apparatus, spare lamps should be in stock. The apparatus should not be moved when hot, thus lengthening the life of the lamp. Lenses and mirrors should be cleaned with lens paper as frequently as those of monocular microscopes.

Note: for elementary work 2 X 2" photomicrographs are preferable to projected prepared slides, and make a micro-projector unnecessary.

An attachment can be bought for the Aldis 500 projector which converts it into a microprojector. Although not so good as a purpose built microprojector, the low cost of the apparatus makes it suitable for elementary classes.

It is possible to line up an ordinary microscope and the light beam of a slide projector, the whole functioning as a microprojector. The monocular microscope has its mirror removed, and is tilted back through 90°. The beam of light from the slide projector is aligned with the condenser (if any) of the microscope, first removing the projection lens from the slide projector.

2. *Slide projectors*

Uses: Projecting 2 X 2" slides of photomicrographs or macroscopic specimens. Most have a film strip attachment and can also be modified for live small aquatic organisms, and as a micro-projector. (see Fig. 4)

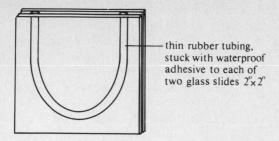

Fig. 4 A live tank

Note that shadows of the object will be projected. This can be used for *Hydra*, *Gammarus* and similar animals. A commercially produced all-glass tank is available from supply agencies.

Types: The most suitable slide projector for school use has a 500W lamp and a fan cooling system. A film strip attachment is a desirable extra, though many filmstrips owned by a school are best cut and mounted as separate slides. The additional refinements of automatic changing of slides and cassette loading are not usually justified for school use.

Materials: 2 × 2″ slides are available from supply agencies for both microscopic preparations and large size specimens. Teachers' own slides are often useful, and photographs of the microscope slides in stock in school can be made if a suitable camera is available. *Nuffield O level Biology Teachers' Guide V,* pp. 54—57 has full information of apparatus and methods for preparing photomicrographs on 35mm film.

Local photographers are often able to make photomicrographs, though the school may have to lend a microscope. Slides of ecological areas and the organisms to be found there are a good introduction to field studies, and slides of unobtainable material and non-indigenous species are also useful.

The present increase in the amount of material available as 2 × 2″ slides, and the reduction in cost of transparencies and duplicates, suggests that use of photomicrographs may be preferable to individual microscope work for elementary classes. The technique of using a microscope is not especially valuable to the average citizen, and in any case what is seen is an image of the real thing. It is obviously much easier to point out features of interest in projected material.

Motile micro-organisms are the exception—it is much more interesting to see a live Amoeba rather than a slide or a photograph of a fixed and stained specimen. But observation of such live material can form part of a 'circus' and in this case one or two microscopes only will be required.

3. Film Projectors

A. 8mm loop projectors

Use: 8 mm film loops, in a loading cassette, run for 3—6 minutes. They illustrate a single concept, or a process or a laboratory technique, and are often as valuable as a full length film (many of which include far too much material). At quite a reasonably low cost, a school can build its own library of these films. The projector is easily loaded, and can be operated by pupils. The loops can be viewed in shaded daylight, using a daylight screen.

Types:
    (i) A projector to use with a separate daylight screen. This is the most easily portable.
   (ii) A projector in a cabinet with an integral daylight screen. This is the standard model, and, though heavy, is as portable as a television receiver which it resembles in appearance.

Materials: A wide range of films are available. The Nuffield and B.S.C.S. courses have sets of these 8 mm loops produced specifically for the course concerned, though they are also of general application.

Teacher's own 8 mm film can be processed and mounted in standard cassettes. Film of ecological areas to be studied can usefully be made if a cine camera is owned or can be borrowed.

B. 16mm sound/silent projectors

Use: The projection of full length sound or silent film.

Types: The modern projector has automatic threading and a built in sound system. Additional loudspeakers and special lenses are available for larger audiences. Older types of projector have separate speakers and often a separate transformer. Threading was not automatic, though a diagram can be found printed inside the case of all standard projectors.

Films can be used to introduce or revise a topic, to show material not available in the locality, and to show processes. Many films use animated diagrams or time-lapse photography. Teachers should remember that a film represents the producer's idea of how the material is to be taught, and all films are not of equal value.

Films should be seen through before being used in class, so that they can be properly introduced. In many cases it is possible to set questions which have to be answered by the class after they have seen the film. Some films can simply be shown—their quality is so good that any additions by the teacher would reduce their impact. In these cases there must be a discussion after the film—few take longer than a single lesson, so there is adequate time for discussion. Where pupils are using English as their second language, the sound commentary may be too rapid for their comprehension, and in such cases it is advisable to run the film silently, adding suitable commentary and explanations.

While the film projector is fairly straightforward to use, it is recommended that the would-be operator should receive both instruction and practice first. The member of the school staff responsible for the visual aid equipment will provide the necessary instruction in its use.

It must be remembered that films are expensive and can easily be damaged by incorrect handling. Therefore time should be spent reading the instruction book provided with the projector. Some common faults may occur when showing a film, however, such as:

a) **Indistinct sound.** The film is threaded too loosely round the sound drum. To remedy, tighten the film between the sound drum and rear take-up sprockets.

b) **Film jumps or flickers on the screen.** Either or both of the loops above and below the gate have been lost. This is usually caused by torn or worn sprocket holes in the film. Stop the projector immediately and rethread. Most modern projectors now have automatic loop formers.

c) **Film breaks.** Should the film break, do *not* attempt to rejoin it with glue, sellotape or metal staples. Run sufficient film through the projector to enable it to be wound round on to the take up spool; check the threading and proceed with the film. Film libraries will repair and splice the films when they are returned to them. Normally films should be sent back *without rewinding*, as they are checked before re-issue. Broken film indicates a fault in the projector or in threading, and this should be carefully checked. Spare reels of various sizes should be bought with the projector. There are 120m, 240m, 480m capacity spools. Films of these lengths have a running time of approximately 11 minutes, 22 minutes and 44 minutes. Select the same size spool for taking up the film as the one which contains the film being shown. They can then be sent back in the container supplied, without rewinding.

As with any projected material, the image is inverted. Titles at the front of the film indicate the correct positioning before threading, and if the threading diagram is followed there should be no problems. While silent films can be used on a sound projector *never* try to use a sound film on a silent projector. The second set of sprockets will damage the soundtrack.

Projectors need to be regularly overhauled by the manufacturer or his agent. Spare lamps and belts should be stocked, and the film gate regularly cleaned with the brush provided. Moving parts need a trace of oil from time to time.

Materials: Films are available from industrial firms and educational agencies. A full list of films and filmstrips available in the United Kingdom is contained in the catalogues of the Educational Foundation for Visual Aids. Films are listed by subject, together with a brief description of content, time, whether sound or silent, colour or black and white, and the age range for which the film is suitable.

Some firms supply film on free loan, though the school pays the postage involved. Local Education Authorities may stock films in regular use as the cost is too great for a school to keep its own stock. In overseas countries, the information offices of the various Embassies and High Commissions have loan libraries of film from their own countries.

Screens: Any white, matt surface is suitable for front projection (i.e. projection towards the side viewed by the audience). The expensive glass beaded models can be seen over a wide angle, but this is not necessary in schools. A flat wall painted with emulsion is perfectly satisfactory. If a portable screen is required, choose the most robust in relation to cost.

Daylight screens are not generally suitable for 16mm film, except for small groups. Daylight screens normally have the image projected on to the back of the surface viewed—as in a television receiver, which has a daylight, back projection screen.

4. *Overhead projectors*
Use: In place of blackboard work. The projector is placed on the desk
in front of the teacher, and the material (written on a roll of transparent
paper with a special pencil) is projected by an angled mirror to a screen
above and behind the teacher. As the screen has to be fixed, this
projector is best kept in one room. Larger educational establishments
are installing overhead projectors as routine lecture room equipment.
They save a great deal of physical work involved in blackboard writing,
and are especially useful in hot countries—where the amount of blackboard work is greater than normal because of the language problem,
and the energy to write on the board at length proportionally less!
Materials:
   (i) Writing or sketching paper and pencils.
  (ii) Sets of transparencies of standard diagrams. Some of these are
        a series of outlines which may be superimposed in sequence to
        built up a complex structure, such as a blood system.
 (iii) Materials for teachers to make their own transparencies,
        consisting of special inks and plastic films about 9″ square—a
        suitable size for projected diagrams.
Care: The reflecting surfaces must be kept free of dust. Spare lamps
should be kept, and, as with other projection equipment, the apparatus
should not be moved whilst hot.

5. *Radio and television programmes*
   Most countries now have a schools broadcasting service, and supply
well-produced notes and illustrative matter for the programmes. Radio
programmes are put on tape for school use, as well as being broadcast
at scheduled times. Television programmes are increasingly available
as 16mm film or as videotape. As with other film, teachers can best
assess the value of a particular programme or series by seeing it prior
to possible class use.
   The future of broadcast programmes probably lies more in the
production of 'programmes' on videotape—the apparatus for reproducing
the programme is not expensive compared with other audio-visual
apparatus, nor are the tapes. It would be quite feasible for a school to
built up its own videotape library in place of frequently hiring film.

6. *Epidiascopes*

These cumbersome machines, having the dual purpose of projecting slides or, by angled mirrors, pages from a book, are not generally bought at the present time. If the school or college has an epidiascope, the projection of diagrams and graphs on to a piece of chart paper enable classroom illustrations to be made easily and quickly, without any skill in drawing being necessary.

7. *Charts*

Charts are large scale illustrations, which can be used in place of, or in addition to, other visual material. Commercially produced charts vary in usefulness. Some have too much detail, others (in particular a set of human anatomy charts) use colours which can only be described as lurid. The most useful are the so-called 'blackboard charts', white outlines on black, of commonly used diagrams such as the mammalian skeleton and blood circulation. They are not labelled, but the surface can be chalked upon and later cleaned.

Charts made in school need to be neat, and clearly labelled. Econasign stencil kits are not cheap, but produce professional results in lettering. Charts which are built up during a sequence of lessons (e.g. an evolutionary time scale and fossil chart) form a useful summary of the main points as the topic progresses. Pupils can contribute to such charts, and in some topics this is the only record necessary.

3.5 Collection and maintenance of living organisms in the laboratory

LABORATORY STOCK

Biology is the study of living organisms, and, with few exceptions, dead and preserved material has no place in a modern biology laboratory. There may be organisms which cannot be obtained locally, and in these cases preserved material has to be used—though often a good colour slide is preferable to a badly preserved, unattractive-looking specimen.

Most of the animals and plants required for elementary work can be kept alive in the laboratory with very little trouble—once the cultures or habitaria are well established. Others can be obtained from the school compound or local habitats, especially in tropical countries where there is a wealth of living material continually available. There is a welcome move to use local specimens for study in most countries.

For many years students were asked to study 'foreign' species, mainly because these were fully identified and described in detail in standard texts. Now that general principles and patterns of structure have replaced detailed study of isolated 'types', any biology teacher should be able to use local materials for their teaching in school.

AQUARIA

A balanced aquarium is a source of:

Protozoa

Flagellates and ciliates are to be found in the mud at the bottom of the tank. These are mostly bacteria feeders, therefore can be cultured in any medium supporting bacterial growth. Hay infusions (about 10 g hay boiled in 1 litre pond water for 30 minutes, and then filtered) can be inoculated with aquarium mud. A boiled cereal grain should be added and changed every week. A suitable container is a McCartney bottle or 3 × 1″ specimen tube, with 1−2 ml medium at the bottom. A large quantity of medium in a container obviously makes it difficult to locate the organisms.

Teachers may care to try the following methods, which are less orthodox but generally more successful.

a) Chop a few inches of herbaceous stem from a plant having plenty of sap, for example dahlia, lily, iris, or, in the tropics, *Canna indica*. Allow to decay a few days, then decant the liquid and inoculate with the organisms. If the stem has been left uncovered, organisms such as *Colpidium sp.* and *Paramecium sp.* may already be present in the medium.

b) Mix 1 g malted milk with 1 litre of water. Boil, or, if possible, autoclave at 15 lbs pressure for 20 minutes. Inoculate with organisms when cool.

Algae

Multicellular algae, once introduced into the tank, grow readily provided there is sufficient light. Desmids, diatoms and green flagellates will be present, but in insufficient numbers to collect for observation. If some of the debris from the bottom of the aquarium is placed in Knop's solution (q.v.) in a jam jar, and kept in strong light, growth of these algae is encouraged, and the water soon becomes a deep green colour. It is as well to set up new cultures every few weeks, and up to six weeks before the material is required.

Invertebrate animals

Snails, insect larvae and small crustaceans can be added from local freshwater habitats, as well as the remains of any live cultures bought from supply agencies. Hydra can be established in a laboratory aquarium; *Hydra viridis* seems to be the easiest to establish.

Fish

A number of small fish, which breed rapidly, are much more useful than a small number of ornamental goldfish. A general rule is 'one inch of fish to a gallon of water', but this can be exceeded if the water is aerated, and if small fish are kept—obviously the rule applies to the volume of fish rather than the length!

Guppies (*Lebistes reticulatus*) survive in warm climates or in a normally heated laboratory without any aquarium heating. They can be used for life cycle studies as well as structure, respiration experiments, and the observation of blood circulation. In temperate climates sticklebacks provide material for studies of territorial behaviour. One male per tank is the rule, unless tanks larger than 2' 6" long are available.

Higher plants

Aquatic flowering plants are necessary to keep an aquarium aerated. In addition, floating duckweeds are useful for growth and mineral deficiency experiments, and submerged plants for photosynthesis studies. *Elodea sp.* and related genera have leaves containing relatively large chloroplasts, which can be observed in a leaf viewed by a microscope, without tedious extraction from ground material.

Setting up an aquarium

Any large container is suitable. Metal framed glass tanks are the most durable, though the smaller sized plastic tanks now available are cheaper and can be bought in greater quantities where funds are limited. Miniature aquaria can be set up in jam jars, failing any other container. The most important requirement is that the water surface is large, relative to the volume. Balanced aquaria have been successfully maintained in plastic washing-up bowls, now obtainable cheaply all over the world.

All aquaria need a raised glass or heavy duty polythene cover, to cut down evaporation and exclude dust. Pond water or rain water should be used. Chemically treated tap water can be used if it is left to stand for a week or so before living material is added. The excess chlorine diffuses out during this time. Washed sand and/or gravel is suitable for rooting plants and providing shelter for small animals. A few scrubbed stones give shelter for larger animals.

Plants and a small amount of mud from a natural pond should be added about three weeks before animals, and fish thrive better if they are added after the aquarium has become established (about 6–8 weeks). The water should not need changing. A piece of animal charcoal floating on the surface seems to keep an aquarium in good condition. If there is too much algal growth, it is necessary to cut down the incident light.

Aquarium accessories

An aerator pump supplying a series of aquaria is useful, and even the cheapest gives sufficient pressure to supply 5 or 6 diffusers. Heaters are not normally required for school tanks, and special lighting is only really necessary in countries having a long dark winter—when aquaria tend to become unbalanced due to a low rate of plant growth.

PLANT MATERIALS
Flowering plants
Uses: physiology experiments, study of life cycles, anatomy and morphology studies. Pelargoniums are easily propagated from cuttings, and therefore have been a popular laboratory plant for many years. Useful as they are, thin leaved plants such as *Coleus sp.* are better for photosynthesis work, and also occur in variegated form for chlorophyll studies. They are easily raised from seed. *Zebrina sp.* are readily propagated from cuttings, and have variegated leaves.

Life cycles

Most of the common annuals normally grown in gardens lend themselves to study of a complete life cycle. They can be grown in the biology garden, or in good potting compost in plant pots, in a Wardian case. Suitable plants for temperature climates are antirrhinium, cineraria, dwarf sweet peas, and even varieties of peas and beans. Many seed firms sell unusual varieties of common plants, easy to grow and interesting to observe. It is quite possible to follow through a plant life cycle from germination to seed and fruit formation, and much more meaningful than studying each stage of growth in isolation.

Plant Anatomy

Helianthus annuus has become the standard 'type' specimen for elementary plant anatomy studies. There is no real reason why this should be so. Material to grow for sectioning as fresh material includes maize, beans, sycamore (which germinates only too readily from seeds), and the new growth occurring in spring from dormant twigs such as horse chestnut. These latter can be collected around February and will sprout in a warm laboratory in two weeks or so.

In all these cases, stem structure can be related to leaf arrangement seen in the living plants—far better than an unrelated pattern in a prepared transverse section of an unfamiliar plant.

Plant responses

For light and gravity responses, oat coleoptiles are the obvious choice. For responses to water, mustard or cress roots give a noticeable response to an atmosphere dried with silica gel. Sensitive plants, especially *Mimosa pudica* are easy to grow, and seeds are sold by most large suppliers.

Genetics

Albino tobacco and tomato seeds are available from biological supply agencies, as first crosses to produce 3:1 Mendelian ratio when germinated. In the tropics, coloured maize can be bought in markets, and cross-pollinated to produce cobs of mixed coloured grains. Cross-pollination in maize merely involves removing the male inflorescence of the plants from which pollen is *not* to be used in the particular cross. The inflorescence should be removed as soon as it appears on the plant, well before pollen is formed. Hybrid cobs can be bought as demonstration material from supply agencies.

Succulents and cacti

A selection of these plants illustrates adaptations to water shortage. They are best bought from horticultural suppliers. They should be included in work on the relative amounts of water transpired—succulents in particular give interesting results.

Mosses, liverworts and ferns

A stock of these can be kept in an old aquarium tank. A three inch layer of potting compost, preferably collected from the plant's natural habitat, kept damp and shaded from direct sunlight, supports the growth of most species of lower plants. Bryophytes do seem to favour a quite specific pH, and it is best to have varieties from one habitat only in the tank.

Germination

Maize and various species of bean have been used for many years in germination experiments, to demonstrate different types of seedling development. In addition, it is interesting to grow local wild plant seeds, including estimates of per cent viability as well as observing the type of germination. In the tropics ground nuts germinate readily, and Bengal green gram (Mung or Moong beans in the U.K.) germinates within 24 hours in a warm atmosphere. The latter is especially useful for experiments on germination conditions, as results are rapidly obtained.

ANIMAL MATERIAL

Mammals

The Universities Federation for Animal Welfare publishes a book *Animals in Schools*[1], giving full instructions for keeping small mammals. If these conditions of housing and feeding cannot be easily maintained, then it is better not to attempt to keep these animals in the laboratory.

Black and white mice can be temporarily kept for genetics experiments—their novelty will ensure they are looked after properly for some weeks. The plastic cages with metal grid covers on sale from all supply agencies are the most suitable and easiest to clean. Proprietary food pellets give a balanced diet, without the risk of overfeeding protein and the resultant smell from the animals. Sawdust is not the best litter—a thin layer of sand is preferable, and must be regularly changed.

Where an animal room is available, a selection of small mammals is invaluable in life history studies. In city schools the laboratory animals may be the only ones many pupils have the chance to see and handle, and are worth keeping for that reason alone.

Birds

Attracting local species by providing a bird table and water, in view of the laboratory or in the biology garden, is much better than keeping caged birds in the laboratory. In addition to encouraging a wrong attitude—keeping animals under less than ideal conditions—the birds tend to be noisy and when caged are of little interest.

Reptiles

In countries where lizards are common, there is no need to attempt to keep them in the laboratory. They can easily be collected when required for experiment or dissection in the cool early morning, when they are torpid. There seems little point in keeping caged snakes in any country, and in temperate countries reptiles being uncommon have few uses in elementary courses.

Amphibians

Beyond the tadpole stage, kept in the aquarium, amphibians do not thrive in the laboratory. Even at the late tadpole stage, they should be fed on small pieces of meat or earthworm. Frogs need to be supplied with insects or meat, and are often reluctant to feed at all unless the food is made to move across their line of vision, as would their normal insect food. After the novelty of inducing frogs to eat 'moving food' has worn off, laboratory stock tends to die of slow starvation. It is therefore better to leave amphibians in their natural surroundings, except when used for a few days only in the laboratory, and then released.

Fish

See 'Aquaria', p.71.

Insects

Stocks of cockroaches are easily kept in an old aquarium tank or similar container. They require little special food, thriving on dry bread, biscuits or any cellulose material. The container needs a layer of sawdust, which should be changed every few weeks, though look out for egg cases and replace these in the insect container.

Locusts can be reared in the special cages supplied commercially, or in any container which can be maintained at about 30°C; the best means of heating being an electric light bulb, adjusting the ventilation and using different wattage lamps until the requisite temperature is obtained. Any container which can be so heated, and well ventilated, is suitable. Tubes of sand, 3—4 inches deep, are necessary for eggs to be laid. As young locusts hatch, they can be transferred to a larval cylinder. There is then less competition for food. Fresh grass or soft leaves must be supplied to adults and nymphs daily.

Insect larvae can be reared in cylinders, provided the food plant on which they were found is supplied daily in fresh condition. Larval cylinders can be obtained or improvised. Lepidopteran caterpillars can be left in the cylinder when they pupate, and many emerge as the imago quite successfully. (Figs. 5, 6)

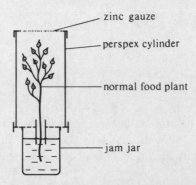

Fig. 5 Larval cylinder—standard

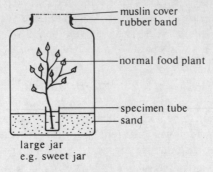

Fig. 6 Larval cylinder—improvised

MATERIAL FROM SUPPLY AGENCIES

Ordering

Biological supply agencies send catalogues and price lists free on request for school use. Details of the specimens available and the amount of time required before material can be supplied is stated in these catalogues. In general, it is as well to ensure that live material is not posted over a weekend, for although most organisms survive several days in good condition, the shorter the time they are deprived of air and subjected to unpredictable temperatures the better.

Fresh material
Treatment on arrival

1. *Protozoa*

Aerate the culture by passing air through with a drawn out dropping pipette. Keep cool, by placing in a water jacket (the simplest way is to float the culture tube in a large beaker of water) if the laboratory is very warm. Avoid extremes of temperature.

2. *Hydra*

Aerate the culture as above, and transfer to a larger container of boiled and cooled pond or rain water. Feeding with hatched brine shrimp eggs keeps the animals in an active condition. Brine shrimp eggs can be hatched by placing a pinch of salt and a pinch of the eggs in 5 ml water.

3. *Flatworms*

Transfer to a larger container of boiled and cooled pond water. Feed on fresh chopped earthworm, removing uneaten food at the end of each day. Flatworms are very sensitive to sudden changes of temperature, and their container should be surrounded by a water jacket.

4. *Algae*

Treat green flagellates as for 'Protozoa'. Transfer larger green algae to a container of Knop's solution, and keep in a good light.

Seaweeds, if not to be used at once, are best allowed to dry out. They can be damped down when required, though if the specimens were obtained for reproductive organs, they should be used within a day or two, storing in a plastic bag to keep the plants wet.

5. *Cockroaches*

See p.76. If the insects are to be dissected within a day or two, they can be placed in a covered small aquarium tank or plastic box, and fed on dry bread, biscuit crumbs, or even filter paper soaked in glucose or sucrose solution.

6. *Small mammals*

Usually these are sent in a suitable container. The animals should be cleaned out, fed and supplied with fresh water on arrival. If required for dissection, they should be starved for a day before killing (see p.75).

Preserved material

Material which is not readily obtainable all the year round may be supplied preserved such as Spirogyra conjugating, Hydra with buds or reproductive organs. It is cheaper to buy material in this form for study than prepared microscope slides. In overseas countries it is worth while considering making one's own permanent slides of material of this type, which merely require staining and mounting.

Some dissection material, mammals, amphibians and fish, can be supplied preserved in embalming fluid (much less objectionable than formalin). These specimens can also be obtained injected to show up the blood system, thus facilitating dissection of these structures.

Subculturing material

It is rarely worthwhile subculturing material which is readily available from suppliers—though Science Club members are often interested in trying to make cultures. Protozoa can be inoculated into any of the media mentioned on p.71. Freshwater aquatic organisms remaining in cultures should not be thrown away, but added to the aquarium stock.

Dissection material

Freshly killed specimens are best for initial dissection, though for later work the embalmed specimens from supply agencies are better than those preserved in formalin in school. Small vertebrates can be killed with ether, chloroform or coal gas. For the latter, special killing boxes are available. A gas supply is led through the container, and out at a point where it can be burnt away.

Animals to be killed in ether or chloroform should be placed in a container with a lid. A small amount of anaesthetic, soaked into cotton wool, is placed in the container with the animals, and the lid left partly open. When the animals are anaesthetized, more ether is added and the container firmly closed. The animals are killed by a high concentration of the chemicals. Earthworms and cockroaches are best killed by a quick dip into almost boiling water—too long in hot water softens the internal tissues.

PREPARATION OF SPECIMENS

(i) Skeletons and teeth

a) In temperate climates, it is necessary to remove flesh from bones by boiling and scraping the animal. In the tropics, the whole animal can be buried in the ground, about 20 cm deep. Marauding ants efficiently remove flesh within a week or so.

b) The bones or teeth may be bleached in 5 vol. hydrogen peroxide, or dried in the sun. In sun-dried bones bleaching occurs at the same time. Skulls and other valuable bones are best dehydrated in a series of alcohols from 30% to 100%, in 10% steps, followed by two changes of xylol.

(ii) Insects

a) Insects can be killed in ethyl acetate vapour, or the vapour of a standard insecticide. (DDT and similar compounds are banned in most countries—pyrethrum based insecticides are judged to be ecologically safe). Cyanide killing bottles are not suitable for schools.

b) Relaxing fluid can be obtained from supply agencies, and facilitates setting of the insect. It is not essential.

c) Setting boards can be obtained from supply agencies or made in school. They provide a means of setting the wings flat and open by placing the abdomen in a groove. The simplest setting board is made by sticking two match box covers to a piece of stiff cardboard, to provide the cross-sectional shape shown in Fig. 7. Insects are set in place by strips of paper pinned across the wings. (Fig. 8)

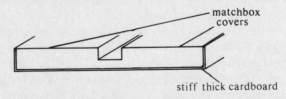
matchbox covers

stiff thick cardboard

Fig. 7 Improvised setting board

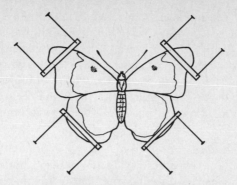

Fig. 8 How to set a butterfly

After a week or so, the insect may be transferred to a permanent collection box, a pin and label placed through the abdomen. The label should show the identification of the insect, and where and when collected.

Closed cases are best for storage, and a few crystals of p-dichlor-benzene in the container prevents destruction by ants and similar insects.

(iii) Herbarium specimens

A reference collection of common plants is essential in the developing countries, where the flora is not yet well known. Small collections are useful in all countries when they are taken from ecological areas which are studied from year to year.

a) Where the plant is small enough, stem, root, upper and lower leaves, flowers and fruits should all be represented on the specimen taken. Specimens are dried in a plant press, between sheets of paper (newspaper) which are changed daily for the first few days. Commercially made presses are of heavy wire mesh, held together by strong springs. Presses can be made in school from two rectangles of wood, held at the corners with nuts and bolts. (Fig. 9)

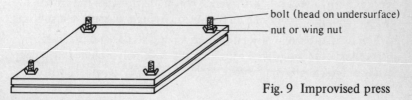

bolt (head on undersurface)
nut or wing nut

Fig. 9 Improvised press

b) When dry, the specimen is mounted on herbarium paper, or any reasonably heavy paper. The label should show the name of the plant, its family, when, where and by whom collected.

Herbarium specimens can be preserved by spraying with 0·1% mercuric chloride solution, to prevent the growth of fungi, or with a proprietary anti-mould preparation. Spraying with insecticide at regular intervals, or storing with p-dichlor-benzene prevents attack by insects.

(iv) Plastic embedding

Small, delicate specimens, providing they are dry, can be embedded in a polymer obtainable with full instructions from supply agencies. Commercially made specimens are useful as class specimens, as damage is minimal and the transparent resin enables all-round viewing of the material.

(v) Plaster casts

In addition to models of certain structures, casts of fossils are obtainable from supply agencies. The fossil horse sequence, reconstructions of humanoid skulls, and primitive bird fossils are the most useful. A representative collection of common fossils—trilobites, graptolites, ammonites—can also be obtained.

3.6 Laboratories in the tropics

DETERIORATION OF MATERIAL

Wood is susceptible to attack by termites and by moulds. Cupboards, especially near sinks where conditions are more humid, need to be regularly inspected and sprayed with an insecticide. Note that DDT is now banned in most countries, and pyrethrum based insecticides are being produced once more.

Floors are usually of concrete, and benches are often supported on brick blocks rather than on a wood frame. Regular cleaning of wooden benches with linseed oil, or a silicone polish, discourages the growth of moulds, and prevents drying out, with consequent warping and splitting.

Iron or steel used in dissecting tools, clamp stands and the like, rusts quickly unless covered with a substance which excludes air. Clamp stands, rings, clamps and bosses should be regularly repainted with zinc paint.

Dissecting instruments need to be carefully cleaned and dried after use, and covered with a film of grease. Wiping with a duster soaked in a cheap local oil—groundnut, corn oil, coconut oil as available—seems to prevent rust in tools which are regularly used. Storage for any length of time should be in a desiccator, or a tin containing silica gel, and sealed with sellotape.

Rubber hardens and perishes at high ambient temperatures. Synthetics, such as neoprene or polythene should be used wherever possible. Most U.K. suppliers stock neoprene bungs, and plastic tubing is obtainable everywhere.

Paper, when it becomes damp, is subject to attack by moulds which digest the cellulose. (The same mould will live on cotton fabrics.) Books must be regularly inspected and in very humid and warm climates should be in a cupboard having a low wattage enclosed element electric heater (of the type fitted in clothes cupboards in the tropics).

Cockroaches and several species of beetle will consume paper, so regular spraying with an insecticide is essential. Herbarium specimens will not be attacked by moulds if they are sprayed with a 0·1% solution of mercuric chloride.

Lenses of microscopes, projectors, cameras, especially if coated with a gelatine film, must be kept in a desiccator to prevent attack by moulds. Once the mould is established, there is no alternative but to have the lens reground or replaced—both costly processes.

When microscopes are in constant use, a packet of silica gel inside the case is sufficient to keep the atmosphere dry—provided the gel is dried out as soon as the colour change indicates it to be damp (silica gel is mixed with cobalt chloride, changing therefore from blue to pink when it becomes damp). During vacations, lenses must be removed and stored in a desiccator, after inspection and cleaning.

Regular cleaning of all lenses discourages fungal growth, and polishing with lens paper which have been impregnated with a proprietary 'anti-mould' preparation helps prevent fungal growth.

Museum specimens. Cockroaches and ants are a constant hazard, especially in insect collections. Para-dichlor-benzene, obtainable from most chemists, should be placed in each container and replaced as it evaporates.

Preserved specimens do not stay in good condition, and if preserved material must be used, the plastic mounts in which the material is embedded in transparent resins are more satisfactory than liquid preservatives.

Chemicals

Volatile liquids and inflammable liquids need to be kept in a cool dark store-room. They should be purchased in small quantities as suppliers usually have better storage facilities than schools.

Enzymes deteriorate quickly, and stocks need to be replaced about every six months.

Many *stains* are best made up or purchased as required, as decomposition of large stocks is wasteful. Most stains used in elementary work can be readily made up in school.

Poisons need to be both clearly labelled and very carefully locked away, as do corrosive liquids. A proportion of the population, especially junior staff employed in cleaning the laboratory, are unlikely to be able to read English. It is therefore necessary to ensure that no potentially dangerous materials are left about the laboratory, labelled or not!

STOCK MAINTENANCE

Most countries now have supply agencies, who keep routine equipment in stock. However, unusual items have to be imported, and this can take up to six months from the date of ordering. It is therefore necessary to maintain rather more spare stock than is usual in industrial countries. If the stock book has been properly kept, it will be possible to estimate a year's supply of consumables, and plan accordingly. Spares such as projector lamps should be duplicated, so there is always at least one in hand.

Repairs

Capital equipment needs to be regularly overhauled, and suppliers generally have local agents who are authorized to carry out repairs and maintenance. However, the instruction book supplied with any piece of apparatus should be carefully kept. It is frequently quicker and less hazardous for the teacher to carry out simple repairs and maintenance, however enthusiastic and confident local 'experts' may be. Most equipment used in biology is simple enough to be understood by anyone with a scientific training.

Stocks of chemicals which deteriorate should not be unduly large. Standard chemicals are more readily available than items of apparatus. If chemicals have to be imported, care must be taken to order dry stains etc., and undiluted liquid. There is a popular story in the tropics of a chemistry teacher who imported a dozen W. Qts. of N/100 sulphuric acid, at great expense.

LABORATORY WASTES

Chemical wastes are generally led into a soak-away or septic tank which is quite separate from domestic waste tanks, the reason being that many chemicals would interfere with the proper functioning of a domestic septic tank. If the teacher has any hand in the design of a laboratory, this should be explained to the architect.

Waste animal material quickly becomes noxious in the tropics. Incineration is the best method of disposal, but if this is impracticable material can be buried in a deep pit and covered with earth. A deep pit prevents marauding animals digging up the remains of dissected materials. Ants and other soil invertebrates quickly dispose of flesh—if skeletons are required the simplest method of cleaning is to bury the dead animal and leave the ants to clean it up for about six weeks.

LIVING MATERIAL

Local specimens

All the living material mentioned in section 3.5 can be kept in the laboratory in the tropics. In addition, there will be an abundance of living material just outside the laboratory, whether or not a biology garden is maintained. For many years, foreign species have been set on the syllabi for public examinations, and few teachers objected as these species were described in detail in standard texts. Local variations in 'type' specimens were ignored—if indeed the actual organisms were collected and examined. There is nowadays a welcome tendency for examination boards to be less specific in their requirements for study of particular specimens. Although naming a specimen is not important in itself, accurate identification makes for ease of reference. It is possible to identify most invertebrate animals as far as the genus (or class in the case of insects) by using a standard key from Europe or America. For use by pupils, the Nuffield *Key to small organisms etc.* [2] and the *Key to pond organisms* [3] are of general use throughout the world.

If more precise identification is required, national museums of natural history or university departments should be approached. New species are continually being discovered, and biology teachers should be aware of the possibility of finding a 'new' species.

Mammals

Small mammals such as mice and rabbits can be kept in the tropics. An outside shelter, well shaded, is preferable to an animal room. It is not advisable to try to tame wild mammals such as monkeys and antelope. They are usually subject to too much attention in school and it is difficult to prevent children feeding the animals with totally unsuitable delicacies.

Freshwater biology

Because of the high incidence of Bilharzia worms (*Schistosoma mansoni*) in freshwater habitats, field work in this area is not advisable. However an artificial pond, protected from pollution, can be dug near the laboratory and stocked with specimens from nearby ponds. Care should be taken when collecting to wear rubber gloves, and not to wade in the water without protective boots or waders. Freshwater organisms are of such interest, it is a pity to ignore them altogether because of the hazard of Bilharzia. A well stocked artificial pond and some aquaria in the laboratory, once established, will provide sufficient material for study.

Uses of local organisms

A list of organisms abundant in the tropics, together with their uses follows:

Protozoa Paramecium, Colpidium and Vorticella occur commonly in fresh water ponds, and can be cultured in the laboratory as described on p. 71. The cultures must be kept very cool.

Algae can be obtained and cultured as described on p. 71.

Mosquitoes can be reared in a tank of pond water in the laboratory. The tank must be covered with mosquito netting, and the imagos destroyed as soon as they have been used for observation. In most areas it is only necessary to leave the water tank in a dark corner of the laboratory for 24 hours or so—after which eggs can be observed on the surface.

Locusts can be reared in a ventilated glass or metal container (having a glass front or lid). A 3–4 inch layer of sand encourages egg laying. Any local species of grasshopper can be kept and all should be provided with fresh grass or leaves daily. None should be allowed to escape.

Termites collected from a nearby termite mound are useful in response experiments. They can be returned to their natural habitat after use.

Ants show response to humidity, and also are quite selective in their food requirements. 20 or more ants in a small container with flour, sugar or chalk (or any other material the class may suggest!) show a definite preference for one material.

Cockroaches can be kept for life cycle and metamorphosis studies.

Reptiles, notably *lizards*, provide material for the study of vertebrates in general. They are good for dissection, being relatively free of fat. The species of *Agama* in particular establish well defined territories and thus are useful for behaviour studies. They are easily caught in the early morning, when still torpid, and can then be marked for identification purposes. There are two useful texts on the structure and habits of the Rainbow Lizard (*Agama agama var. agama*) by Harris[4] & [5].

Flowering plants are more easily identified than many animals. Most countries now have a local flora, and museums have herbarium collections to assist identification. Small plants, for example the ubiquitous *Tridax procumbens*, are useful for photosynthesis experiments, as well as for observation of structure and life cycle. Specimens should be collected just before the lesson as most wild flowers wilt very quickly. Plants to grow in the biology garden include:

Hybrid maize—for genetics demonstrations.
Canna indica—for monocotyledonous insect pollinated flowers.
Salvia spp.—for the pollination mechanism.
Coleus hybrids—for photosynthesis (variegated leaves).
Hibiscus spp. for large flowers (and attracting sunbirds!)
New varieties of local crop plants to show methods of crop improvement. Agricultural officers are only too ready to help with these, to publicize their availability.

Non-flowering plants can be kept in the laboratory in a container of damp compost. Mosses can be found in rain forest though ferns and liverworts are more abundant in cloud forest at high altitudes. Stock may be obtained from a university botany department, and grows best in cool shady surroundings.

No examination syllabus should demand study of an organism which is not locally obtainable. Teachers are at liberty to write to examination boards to suggest the substitution of local specimens, and should not hesitate to do so. It is usually lack of knowledge of local specimens by the examining authority which causes retention of foreign species on a syllabus.

3.7 Laboratory Technicians

A well trained laboratory technician is an integral part of a teaching team. Larger schools are usually fortunate in having several laboratory assistants, headed by a fully qualified technician. Smaller schools may have less qualified assistance and many have only unqualified personnel whose training rests with the head of department.

Whatever the level of training of technicians, the final responsibility for the smooth running of a laboratory and the provision of materials for practical lessons rests with the teacher. The amount of responsibility delegated to technicians depends upon their level of training and experience. Young teachers and students do tend to rely far too much on technicians, and they are far too often blamed for the 'failure' of an experiment on teaching practice.

Teachers must check the materials they have ordered well before the lesson, so that mistakes can be rectified. New types of apparatus and materials must be fully explained to technicians and it is often necessary for a teacher to prepare such new materials himself the first few times they are used.

Duties delegated to technicians
Technicians can be expected to:

1. Maintain the laboratory and contents in good condition, notifying caretaker of defects in fittings and services.
2. Set up apparatus and provide materials from stock for lessons, as requested by teaching staff.
3. Collect live materials from local habitats.

4. Dismantle, clean and store away apparatus after a lesson. (Junior staff are often provided in larger schools for routine apparatus cleaning.)
5. Keep stock book and note deficiencies.
6. Keep supply agency catalogues and make out orders for routine replacement of consumables.
7. Keep a breakage record.
8. Maintain stocks of bench reagents.
9. Care for live materials kept in the laboratory and ancillary rooms.
10. Assist in the laboratory during lessons. This too rarely happens, usually because one technician is in charge of several laboratories, and time simply does not permit direct involvement in lessons. Where technicians, even those totally unqualified, can take part in class laboratory work their interest and skills are greatly increased.

Bibliography

1. Animals in Schools. Universities Federation for Animal Welfare. J.P. Volraith. (1956)

2. A Key to Small organisms in soil, litter and water troughs. Nuffield Foundation. Longmans/Penguin.

3. Key to Pond Organisms. Nuffield Advanced Science. Longmans/Penguin.

4. The Anatomy of the Rainbow Lizard. Vernon A. Harris. Hutchinson (1963).

5. The Life of the Rainbow Lizard. Vernon A. Harris. Hutchinson (1963).

See also: Nuffield Secondary Science   Apparatus Guide
Longman/Penguin (1971).

UNESCO Source Book for Science Teaching
Unesco (1967 revised edition)

SCHEMES OF WORK WITH PRACTICAL DETAILS

4.1 Introduction

The following schemes are planned to present the first stages of the learning process, i.e. the aquisition of a knowledge of the basic facts. This leads to an understanding of concepts, and later to problem-solving by the application of fundamental principles. Suggestions are made in some topics for problems which can be set, though in the early stages these must be simple and based on questions asked by pupils wherever possible. It is only realistic to recognize that lower ability groups will not reach the problem-solving stage, though they can be encouraged to seek the answers to their own questions by experimental work and observation. Higher ability groups, through problem-solving, come to realise that there is much that is not yet known or understood in the biological sciences

The *process* of problem-solving is more important than the end result. Opponents of 'new' teaching methods often fail to understand that pupils are not expected to reach research-type conclusions—but they are able to find the answers to such simple questions as, for example, 'How fast does a leaf grow?'

Although the following schemes have been designed so that basic facts can be clearly understood each can and must be presented as a discovery situation. The difference between 'To show that plants need light to photosynthesize' and 'To find out whether plants can make starch in the absence of light' may seem small, but denotes very different approaches to teaching. The former presupposes the result; the latter is open-ended. It is only too easy to forget that whereas the teacher knows the result, the pupils do not!

4.2 The energy changes in living organisms

TYPES OF ENERGY CHANGE

Energy changes can be simply presented as a circus including:

(i) Chemical energy to heat energy
   a) Heat from micro-organisms.

     Set up two conical flasks of $500\,cm^3$ capacity. (Fig. 10) Flask A

contains 5 g fresh yeast or 2 g dried yeast, and a 5% solution of
glucose. Flask B contains the same amount of yeast together
with distilled water in place of the glucose solution.

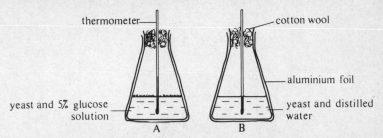

Fig. 10 To show the change from chemical to heat energy

Enclose each flask in aluminium foil to retain any heat produced and plug the flasks loosely with cotton wool, placing a
thermometer in each.

A significant rise in the temperature of flask A indicates that
the presence of glucose enables release of heat energy.

b) Heat from animals.

Set up a differential air thermometer as shown in Fig. 11. In one
tube place six to eight large insects (cockroaches, locusts) or insect
larvae (maggots, caterpillars). The other tube contains dead
material. The liquid in the U-tube can be coloured with eosin.

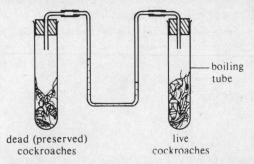

Fig. 11 To demonstrate heat given off by animals

Insect material is better than earthworms (often suggested for
this experiment), as the rate of respiration is higher and thus
results are quicker and more significant.

c) Heat from plant material.

Set up two thermos flasks as shown in Fig. 12. Rinse the seeds in a weak disinfectant solution to kill any surface bacteria (which respire rapidly and give a false rise in temperature in the control apparatus).

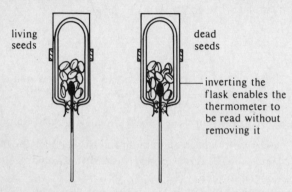

Fig. 12 To demonstrate heat given off by plants

(ii) Chemical energy to kinetic energy

For this it is only necessary to provide examples of animals moving in various ways and in various media. Pupils readily relate the movement of macroscopic animals to energy change, but do not always appreciate that the same applies to microscopic organisms.

The following range of organisms is suggested:

a) Amoeba or ciliates or flagellates on a slide in water without any slowing medium.

b) Nematodes or rotifers, extracted from soil by Baerman funnel method *Nuffield Biology Text IV*, p. 49.[1]

c) Earthworms.

d) Insects.

e) Fish.

f) Small mammals.

g) Film loop (8 mm) of cell division or binary fission in Amoeba, to show movement within a cell, *or* staminal hairs of *Tradescantia* to show streaming cytoplasm.

(iii) Chemical energy to electrical energy

Difficult to show except by pictures and a brief account of the electric ray. It is unlikely that the class will have sufficient knowledge of the functioning of the nervous system for a reference to be relevant at this stage.

(iv) Chemical energy to light energy

Pupils in the tropics will have seen fireflies, and in other areas reference can be made to the planktonic *Noctiluca*, luminescent fungi, and glow-worms. One biology supply agency in the United States sells dried fireflies, which produce light when ATP solution is added. The expense of the insects and of the ATP makes this impracticable for the majority of schools.

(v) Light energy to chemical (or stored) energy

Test extracts of leaves which have been in light and in darkness for the presence of starch. (See p. 94 b) for the extraction method.)

This demonstration presupposes that starch is recognized by pupils as an energy storing compound.

STORING ENERGY

An appreciation of the energy-storing process of photosynthesis involves the adoption of a standard for assuming that the process has taken place. The formation of starch in a leaf of a green plant which has been destarched before exposure to light is the usual standard. It is necessary to *prove* that there is no starch in the plant before assuming it to be destarched. Some plants require as much as three days in total darkness before all starch is translocated from the leaves. Starch testing may be carried out in two ways:

a) Kill a whole leaf, or discs taken from a leaf with a cork borer, or squares cut from a leaf with scissors, and boil the tissue to kill it. Extract the chlorophyll, which masks the starch test colours, by immersing the tissue in warm methylated spirits. When the leaf tissue is cream coloured, rinse it in warm water, and add iodine solution. A blue-black colouration indicates the presence of starch.

Methylated spirits is highly inflammable, and thus small pieces of leaf tissue are preferable to a whole leaf, as the amount of spirit required is reduced. Discs or squares of tissue can be placed in a test tube half full of methylated spirit, and the tube placed in a beaker of hot water.

b) Starch testing is possible without using inflammable solvents if the test is done on an extract of ground leaf tissue in place of leaves or leaf discs.

Grind up the tissues to be tested in a mortar, with water and a little sand. Decant the liquid into a boiling tube, and *boil vigorously for one minute.* This brings any starch present into colloidal solution. Allow the debris to settle, decant and cool the clear liquid, and add iodine solution. Extracts from leaves containing starch show the characteristic blue-black colour.

This test can be adapted for all standard photosynthesis experiments, except in the use of complex stencils in light effects. Even here, it is only necessary to use a complete dark cover over one area of the leaf, and test an extract of this area and an extract from the rest of the leaf separately.

Very rarely, where leaves are very acid, small amounts of starch are hydrolysed in boiling and a negative result is obtained. This happens too rarely to cause any problem at elementary levels.

The process of photosynthesis can be illustrated by the following, arranged as a 'circus' occupying several lessons, or as group work. In the latter case, one experiment will occupy one lesson of about 1¼ hours duration.

(i) The formation of starch in the light.

Destarch a plant by keeping it in a well ventilated dark cupboard *for at least 36 hours.* Test a leaf to find if there is starch present. If there is, it is necessary to return the plant to the dark, until destarching is complete. Treat different leaves of the plant as follows:

a) Stencil part of a leaf with a strip of light-proof paper, making the lower surface covering loose enough to allow air to circulate.

b) Stencil a leaf with a photographic negative on the upper surface, light-proof paper on the lower surface. This gives a range of light intensity.

c) Cover parts of the leaves with 'Wratten' colour filters. The following have been found suitable:

yellow 08, deep red 29, deep blue 47, green 58, and visually opaque infra-red 88.

The filters are obtainable from science supply agencies and photographers. Coloured cellophane paper is not usually optically pure, and gives very misleading results.

Note: a suitable cold light source, enabling photosynthesis experiments to be set up overnight, is described in section 3.1, p. 46.

(ii) The absorption spectrum of chlorophyll.

a) Make a chlorophyll extract by grinding fresh young green leaves with acetone and petrol ether in the ratio 1:10. Project a spectrum, preferably using a prism with a diffraction grating, and view the spectrum through the tube of chlorophyll extract. This is much simpler than projecting the spectrum through the extract, though for a large class this may be preferable.

   A colour slide of the absorption spectrum is available from supply agencies, though the colour rendering is not perfect, especially at the ends of the visible spectrum.

(iii) The constituents of chlorophyll.

Prepare an extract of chlorophyll as above, and treat in any or all of the following ways:

a) Place 2 ml of the extract in a McCartney bottle or glass specimen tube, and add a stick of chalk (not the coated 'dustless' variety). Bands of the four different pigments will separate out by this simple chromatographic method.

b) Substitute a 1 X 5 cm strip of chromatography, filter or blotting paper for the stick of chalk.

c) Place a circle of filter paper on a beaker as shown (Fig. 13). Drop the chlorophyll extract on to the centre of the paper, allowing each to dry before adding a further drop. The pigments separate out in a ring form and are best examined with a hand lens.

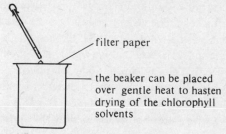

filter paper

the beaker can be placed over gentle heat to hasten drying of the chlorophyll solvents

Fig. 13 To demonstrate the constituents of chlorophyll

d) Take a 1 × 5 cm strip of filter paper, cut to a point at one end. Place a piece of green leaf about 0·5 cm from the pointed end, and hammer it with a scalpel handle or similar instrument until there is a dark green patch of chlorophyll on the paper. Place the paper with the pointed tip just in 1 ml acetone in a specimen tube. The pigments present separate out.

(iv) Chloroplasts.

Look at different chloroplasts in moss leaves, *Spirogyra, Elodea* or *Hydrilla leaves*, and in leaf tissue of land plants pulped with a little sharp sand.

(v) Carbon dioxide and water as raw materials.

The utilization of water cannot be shown in the school laboratory. The use of radio-active tracers could be explained to the more able groups.

Carbon dioxide intake can be shown using Nuffield bicarbonate indicator with land plants or aquatic plants, as shown in Fig. 14.

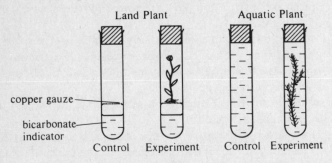

Fig. 14 To demonstrate the intake of CO_2

The need for carbon dioxide in starch formation can be shown by enclosing a leaf of a destarched plant in a carbon dioxide free atmosphere, or by similarly enclosing a whole plant. Small plants such as groundsel or *Tridax* are preferable. Carbon dioxide can be absorbed by soda lime or filter paper soaked in strong caustic soda solution (Fig. 15).

Note that dry soda lime absorbs water, causing stomata to close and hence slowing the rate of photosynthesis (Fig. 16). It is advisable to rinse out the tube with water before assembling the apparatus, to ensure a humid atmosphere.

filter paper
soaked in
NaOH

damp soda lime

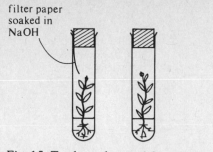

cotton wool

split cork, greased

Fig. 15 To show the need for
CO$_2$ in starch formation

Fig. 16 To show that starch
is not formed in the
absence of CO$_2$.

(vi) Oxygen as a by-product of photosynthesis.

Indigo carmine is decolourized by reducing agents, and the blue
colour is restored in the presence of oxygen. A solution of the indicator
can be just decolourized by adding sodium dithionite, made up as
described in section 3, pp. 57, 61, until the blue colour just disappears.
Immediately add this solution to an aquatic plant in a boiling tube,
filling the tube to the top and closing at once with a well fitting bung.
Set up a similar tube, without the plant, as a control, and a further
tube which is to be kept in complete darkness. Expose the first tube
to light, and note the time for the colour to be restored. (Fig. 14) It is
possible to use the same method with submerged land plants. Keeping
a tube containing the indicator and a plant in the dark is necessary as
some oxygen will be contained in the stomatal spaces, and causes a
slight colour change as it diffuses into the surrounding water.

Analysis of the gas given off by aquatic plants by one of the methods
suggested in section 4 pp. 101, 102, shows a proportion of oxygen greater
than that dissolved in water. There is rarely a sufficient percentage of
oxygen in the mixture to relight a glowing splint. Collecting the gas
in a gas burette rather than in a test tube enables simple analysis. Set
up the apparatus as shown in Fig. 17 overleaf.

RELEASING ENERGY

A standard for the occurrence of respiration is the production of
carbon dioxide. This compound can be tested for with lime water, or

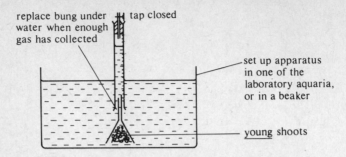

replace bung under   tap closed
water when enough
gas has collected

set up apparatus
in one of the
laboratory aquaria,
or in a beaker

young shoots

Fig. 17 Gathering gas for analysis from aquatic plants

with Nuffield bicarbonate indicator. The latter is by far the more
sensitive of these, and should be used wherever possible. If an
experiment involves the *production* of carbon dioxide only (and not
its removal), then Cresol Red/sodium bicarbonate can be used.

(i) Energy is set free from large molecules

Burn a lump of sugar under a test tube containing 5 ml water. A
little ash mixed with the sugar as it starts to burn absorbs the molten
sugar, which would otherwise extinguish the flame. Water condenses
on the cold tube, and carbon dioxide can be shown by holding a drop
of lime water in a glass tube over the burning sugar. The water
temperature should be taken before and after burning the sugar.

If a calorimeter is available, a variety of substances can be tested,
and a precise estimate of the energy set free can be made. There are
various types of calorimeter on the market, supplied complete with
instructions for use. The 'water equivalent' of the apparatus should be
stated with these instructions—that is, the apparatus heats up as well
as the water jacket, and the energy causing this heating must be
allowed for.

Conversion of kcals to joules.
1 kcal is equivalent to 4185 J.
The table figures are kilojoules (= 1000 J).
For joules add 000 (except for 1 kcal which becomes 4200 and 2 kcal
which becomes 8400).
For numbers less than 1 use the 0—9 row and divide by 10.

For numbers between 100 and 990 use the 10—99 rows and multiply by 10.

	0	1	2	3	4	5	6	7	8	9
0—9	0	4·2	8·4	13	17	21	25	29	33	38
10—19	42	46·0	50·0	54	59	63	67	71	75	79
20—29	84	88·0	92·0	96	100	105	109	113	117	121
30—39	126	130·0	134·0	138	142	146	151	155	159	163
40—49	168	172·0	176·0	180	184	188	192	197	200	205
50—59	210	214·0	218·0	222	226	230	234	238	245	247
60—69	251	256·0	260·0	264	268	272	276	280	284	289
70—79	293	297·0	301·0	305	309	314	318	322	326	330
80—89	335	339·0	343·0	347	351	356	360	364	368	372
90—99	376	380·0	385·0	389	393	398	402	406	410	414

(ii) Living organisms give off carbon dioxide.

It is useful here to refer back to the first experiment on the energy changes listed in 4.1 on p. 90. Yeast produces heat energy only when supplied with glucose, and at the same time produces carbon dioxide. As breaking down glucose by burning also releases carbon dioxide, it can be assumed that yeast is breaking down the same substance.

a) *Carbon dioxide production in animals.*

Set up the apparatus as shown in Fig. 18, using small aquatic and terrestrial animals. Set up a control tube for each case. Try to have equal amounts of material in each tube, and discuss the different rates of colour change.

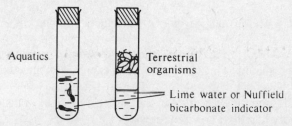

Fig. 18 To demonstrate CO_2 in animals: Control tubes should be set up in each case

b) *Carbon dioxide production in plants.*
The same apparatus as in Fig. 18 is used. Suitable materials are germinating seeds, plant roots and stem and root tubers. It is not wise to include green plants at this stage with lower ability groups, but where they are included, the tubes must be darkened (enclosing in aluminium foil is the simplest way) to prevent the absorption of carbon dioxide during the photosynthetic process.

c) *Carbon dioxide production in micro-organisms.*
Set up a tube containing bicarbonate indicator, a pinch of dried yeast and 5% glucose solution. Set up a control tube without the yeast.

d) *Carbon dioxide production in humans.*
Set up the apparatus shown in Fig. 19. Flask A is the control. Pupils breathe in air through the T-piece and flask A and breathe out via the T-piece and flask B. Alternatively, simply breathe out through a drinking straw into the indicator. As a control use a dropping pipette to pass air through a second tube.

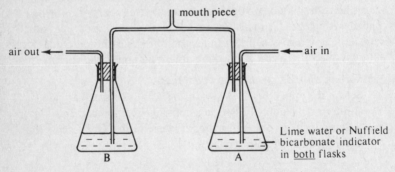

Fig. 19 To demonstrate CO_2 production in humans

Note: Always bring the bicarbonate indicator to equilibrium with the surrounding air before using in an experiment, and avoid breathing out air around the indicator. The air used to obtain equilibrium should be that in the control tubes, the same as that in the laboratory, not from outside.

Quantitative methods of estimating carbon dioxide production
Absorption solutions

Carbon dioxide is readily absorbed by 50% caustic soda solution. Oxygen is absorbed by alkaline pyrogallol. (Which also absorbs carbon dioxide, and must therefore be used for oxygen estimates *after* estimation of CO_2.)

Apparatus

a) Gas burettes—These are graduated tubes, closed at one end with a tap or burette clip, and at the other with a neoprene or rubber bung which remains airtight after piercing with a hypodermic needle. The latter is used to inject the absorption liquids into the tube.

   Burettes can be made from 1 cm glass tubing and the discarded seals from vaccine phials, which are the same as the seals provided with commercially produced gas burettes. Rubber tubing and a burette clip can replace the burette tap. For a full account of the use of gas burettes, see *Nuffield Biology O level Text III*, p. 7.[2] The air to be analysed is collected in the burette, and the absorption fluids are 'injected' into the burette through the seal, using a hypodermic syringe. Reactions must be carried out at a constant temperature by keeping the burettes in a tank of water for a few minutes between each reading. Volumes are measured by opening the tap under water, and allowing water to take the place of the gas which has been absorbed. Tubes can be calibrated by 'Scalafix' tape available from supply agencies, or by marking with a diamond pencil.

   Gas burettes are suitable for the analysis of exhaled air, after activities such as running up stairs, doing a certain number of 'step ups', and comparing the CO_2 content with that obtained at rest. (Fig. 20)

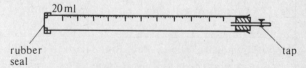

Fig. 20 A gas burette

b) Capillary pipettes—U-shaped capillary tubes fitted with a screw to alter the internal volume enable the analysis of very small air samples. A column of the gas to be analysed is drawn into the tube, and its length noted. The column is then pushed nearly to to the end of the capillary, and caustic soda is drawn in. The 'bubble' of air is moved backwards and forwards several times until there is no further lessening in volume. The new length of the column is noted, and the process repeated with alkaline pyrogallol. (Fig. 21)

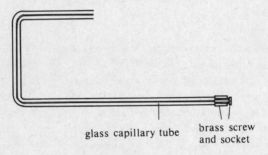

glass capillary tube   brass screw
and socket

Fig. 21 A capillary pipette

If screw-topped pipettes are not available, the end of the pipette can be fitted with a short length of rubber or plastic tubing and a screw clip, the distal end of the rubber tube being sealed with a piece of glass rod. (Fig. 22)

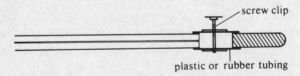

screw clip

plastic or rubber tubing

Fig. 22 An improvised screw top for capillary pipette

Capillary pipettes can be used to analyse the small amounts of gas evolved by aquatic plants, kept in the dark to prevent photosynthesis, as well as the gas evolved during photosynthesis in dull weather—often too small an amount for gas burette analysis.

(iii) Oxygen is used up.

Set up a tube as shown in Fig. 23 with live animals, and a control tube. CO_2 produced is absorbed by a piece of filter paper soaked in saturated potassium hydroxide solution. The rate of oxygen intake can be measured by the rate at which the drop of liquid moves along the capillary tube. If this gets near the end of the tube, add another drop to the end. When there is very slow, or no movement of the drop of liquid, test the gas in the tube with a lighted splint. There will be insufficient oxygen to allow it to burn.

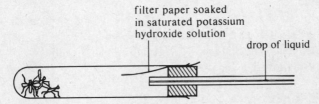

Fig. 23 To demonstrate the rate of oxygen consumption

(iv) Some organisms can respire anaerobically.

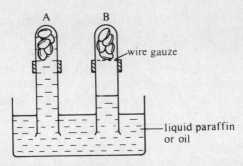

Fig. 24 To demonstrate anaerobic respiration

Tube A contains dry seeds, tube B living seeds, which have been soaked in water. The gas given off by these seeds can be tested with lime water or Cresol Red, and seen to be carbon dioxide.

The demonstration can be set up using mercury as the liquid excluding air, but it should be remembered that mercury is a cumulative poison which can be inhaled as vapour and absorbed through the skin.

Also it is expensive, and not all schools maintain sufficient stocks of it for this type of demonstration.

DEVELOPMENT OF THE TOPIC

Subsequent work related to energy changes may be:

a) Foods and food requirements.
b) Digestion and use of food in animals.
c) Food storage in plants.
d) World food and the problem of supplies with the population explosion.
e) Novel foods and their use in solving world food problems. (See *Food Resources, Conventional and Novel by Pirie*[3].)
f) Applications of genetics to plant and animal breeding.
g) Energy flow in an ecosystem.

PROBLEMS TO SET HIGH ABILITY GROUPS

a) Work out the energy changes when cereal seeds (oats, maize, wheat) are grown in a plastic petri dish, with a weight on the lid. The growing seedlings raise the lid. Try a series of weights with the same number of seedlings, and a series of different numbers and distribution of seedlings with the same weight to raise. Draw attention to plants growing through tarmac and into the foundations of houses.
b) Find out what pigments are present in leaves of copper beech, crotons, coleus. Use the same methods as for the extraction of chlorophyll. Try to find whether chlorophyll is present in petals and red and brown seaweeds.
c) Differentiate the light and dark reactions of photosynthesis by finding whether leaves of destarched plants can manufacture starch in darkness in various concentrations of glucose. Leaf discs give the best results.
d) Make up a series of standards for glucose concentration using Benedict's reagent. Extract the contents of leaf cells and compare the glucose content of leaves from varying light intensities.
e) Compare the rates of carbon dioxide production of standard quantities of different living material. (e.g. 5 g maggots compared with 5 g potato tuber.)

FURTHER INFORMATION
For other experiments and demonstrations for work in energy relationships see:
Nuffield Biology Text and Teachers' Guide III [2]
Nuffield Secondary Science Theme 4 Section 4.2[4]

4.3 Ecological studies

The applications of ecology to food production, pest control and the conservation of our environment need to be continually stressed. Early ecological studies should be in a well defined area, with a *limited number of species*, in order that pupils are not overwhelmed by problems of identification. Ecology is the study of inter-relationships, not the learning of lists of organisms which occur in particular habitats.

A HABITAT IN THE LABORATORY
(i) The laboratory aquarium as an introduction to ecological studies.
Although this will be an artificial habitat, it can be arranged that the species present show a pattern of inter-relationships, which can then be applied in field studies.

The following terms need to be clearly understood:
Habitat—a place where an organism lives, made up of living and non-living factors. The aquarium is a habitat made up of water, with dissolved gases and minerals, a certain pH, temperature and viscosity.
Population—the organisms of one species, living in the same habitat.
Community—the different populations in a habitat. The sum total of all living organisms in the aquarium is the 'aquarium community'.
Ecosystem—a community together with its physical environment, interacting together. The word is obviously derived from 'ecological system'.
Biosphere—the sum total of all ecosystems on our planet.

   a) Distinguish the organisms which are able to photosynthesize, the *Producers* of the aquarium ecosystem.

Plants such as *Elodea* (or *Hydrilla*) and *Vallisneria* are readily identified as plants able to produce food in their green leaves. It is worth while carrying out starch tests on leaves which have been in darkness and in good light for some hours.

Scrape some algae off the tank walls, and take some of the debris at the bottom of the tank. Examine them with a microscope, noting chloroplasts.

b) By observation, notice which animals feed off the plants. Young tadpoles, snails, *Daphnia* and other small crustaceans are *Primary Consumers*. *Detritus* feeders, such as Water Boatmen and many *Dipteran* larvae, consume mainly plant matter, and thus come into the same category.

Use a binocular microscope to observe mouthparts and intestine— or use the live tank of a microprojector.

c) *Dytiscus* beetle larvae are the commonest carnivores, and are best kept separately from the rest of the aquarium animals. The reasons for this should be explained—in an artificial habitat of limited size, even one *Dytiscus* larva would cause havoc. There is scope here for experimental feeding of the larvae, to determine just how much is consumed. *Hydra* is a most useful *Secondary Consumer* to stock in the aquarium, as its feeding can be observed by microprojection. A few brine shrimps, hatched in a separate container and added to the microprojector live tank, are readily captured. *Hydra* will contract when the projector lamp first illuminates it, but, providing it does not get too hot, it will begin feeding in a few minutes.

d) The role of bacteria and fungi as *Decomposers* can be shown:
By culturing a loopful of the debris from the bottom of the tank on nutrient agar. A series of samples from different parts of the aquarium give interesting results. Samples should be removed with a pipette, and transferred to a dish from which loopfuls can be taken for culturing.

A piece of hard boiled egg white, suspended in the aquarium often shows growth of water fungi within a few days. *Saprolegnia* is the commonest, and frequently produces sporangia. The motile spores are useful in later work on dispersal.

The work should be summarized by building up a food web.

(ii) Adaptations to environment

Use a few specific examples, rather than a large number of different types. The aim at this stage is to show what to look for—further examples will be discovered by pupils as the topic progresses.

a) Compare the method of breathing in a land insect with that of an aquatic insect. Water Boatmen compared with Cockroaches, Locusts compared with Diving Beetles are suitably large examples.

Compare also the difference in the ability of the two animals to support their own weight on land.

b) Compare an aquatic plant with a land plant, noting particularly the relative amounts of supporting tissue, subdivision of leaves, cuticularization of leaves and amount of root formation.

In each case the reasons for the differences must be clearly related to properties of water and of air and land as habitats.

(iii) How organisms reach their habitat.

a) *Dispersal methods* in a number of plants and animals can be shown by a 'circus'. The exact organisms used depend upon the locality, but the following is a generalised list which can be collected in most areas, and shows the main dispersal methods:

Encysted *Amoeba*—obtainable as prepared slides.

Spore production in *Mucor*, and in *Saprolegnia.*

Spore print of mushroom or toadstool.

Sporangia of moss, liverwort and ferns. If possible note the dispersal mechanism by means of a microscope.

Seeds and fruits to illustrate wind, water, mechanical and animal dispersal.

In a number of cases, the means of dispersal is also the means of survival of cold and/or dry seasons. Attention should be drawn to this in the work card accompanying each specimen. The vectors of parasites also have a place in this circus.

b) *Response* as a means of reaching and remaining in the habitat. Earthworms, termites, blowfly maggots or woodlice are all excellent material for showing how simple responses keep the animal in the best habitat. Earthworms are the least satisfactory for a series of experiments, as handling quickly causes over-stimulation of the giant fibres and associated neurons, causing inertia.

First define the features of the normal habitat of the animal, and discuss the possible responses necessary to remain in this habitat. Taking one variable at a time, use a choice chamber to investigate the responses selected. Many different kinds of apparatus are described in various laboratory manuals. The simplest is two large test tubes placed end to end, the rims being sealed with plasticine. Dry conditions are obtained with silica gel or calcium chloride granules. Wet cotton wool at the end of the other tube gives a high humidity, and a humidity gradient is established between the extremes within 5 minutes. The tubes can be subjected to varying light intensity, and varying temperatures.

(iv) Colonization of a new habitat, and competition.

a) Make maps to show the different moulds growing on a piece of dampened bread over about ten days. Some will be more successful colonizers than others, leading to the idea of competition for food.

b) Grow bird seed mixture in a seed box of compost (sterilized) in the laboratory. Sow it thickly to cause crowding of the seedlings. Record the species which germinate first, and examine weekly to note changes in the composition of the mixture of plants surviving. A mixture of seeds sold commercially in Britain for winter feeding of garden birds is excellent for this purpose, and cage bird mixtures are also suitable.

c) Clear a plot of ground completely, and remove the top 3″ of soil, which will contain seeds from the plants which were growing in the area. Kept in the laboratory, in seed boxes, this soil shows what seeds survive in the area. Loosen the exposed soil, and record the species which appear in it. This type of long term project can best be carried out in Science Club time.

(v) Ecological survey of a chosen habitat—general plan.

a) Record the location of the site.

b) Record the dimensions of the area.

c) Write a brief general description of the type of habitat, drawing attention to those features most likely to affect the occurrence and distribution of living organisms.

d) Examine the main living organisms, and, by studying their features, group them as producers, consumers, decomposers. List their adaptive features. Try to build up a food web.

e) Soil analysis, of particle size, air and water content, humus content and pH is better dealt with here than as an isolated topic.

f) Work out the distribution of the organisms, and try to relate this to variations in measured light, air currents, soil factors, depth of water in an aquatic habitat. Standard transect and quadrat methods can be used. The transect method of showing uneven distribution seems easier for junior and less able pupils.

g) By seasonal observations, work out the life cycles of a few representative plants and animals. In the case of plants, carry out tests of seed viability by germinating large numbers of seeds in the laboratory. Some animals can be kept in the laboratory for observation, but natural conditions should be reproduced as far as possible, and the animals must be fed regularly.

h) Carry out experiments on the responses of animals to the constant factors in their habitat.

i) In a land habitat, clear a square meter for recolonization observations, as described above.

j) If the area is cut or grazed, grow some of the rosette plants in the laboratory, noting their growth habit when not subject to continual cropping.

k) By reference to the food web, work out the path of energy flow in the system. Fence off a square meter, and take the dry weight of plant material produced in it in a standard time. This gives an approximate idea of productivity.

(vi) Applications of ecological principles—conservation.

a) Biological control of pests comes from a knowledge of the inter-relationships of the organism with others in its natural environment.
  Sometimes a 'foreign' species can be used in control. Suitable examples are the control of rabbits by the myxomatosis virus, and the control of aphids by ladybird beetles. Some of the films on loan from the Shell company include examples of biological control.

b) Control from knowledge of the life cycle, resulting from ecological studies, includes control of the mosquito and the migratory locust. Literature is available from the *Voluntary Committee on Overseas Aid* [7] giving many examples of the uses of ecology in the developing countries, and also sources of more material. Problems of food production, some of which can be solved by the application of ecological principles, are also listed in this source book.

c) Conservation of natural resources, and the reasons for the prevention of pollution are better appreciated when a sound knowledge of ecology has been gained. *Secondary Science Theme 3,*[8] Section 3.5 has excellent material on man's control of his environment.

4.4 Growth, reproduction, genetics and evolution

GROWTH

(i) Growth of a cell.

    a) Grow roots of onion, or better, garlic, by placing bulbs just above water. The roots take from 5–8 days to reach a reasonable length. Cut off about 3 mm root tip, place in water on a slide, and squash by pressing gently on the cover glass. Blot off excess water, and examine the cells, noting how the size varies from the apex backwards. It will be necessary to explain the structure and function of the root cap cells. Iodine can be drawn across the slide to show up cell walls more clearly.

    b) Taking root apices from the same plant, fix in acetic alcohol for 24 hours. Handling the tissue with a brush or section lifter, transfer to N/10 hydrochloric acid at about 60°C for 2–3 minutes. This treatment decomposes the middle lamella, and the cells will separate easily when squashed.

        Place each tip separately on a slide with a drop of aceto-orcein stain. Cut off the first 2 mm with a sharp scalpel or razor blade, and discard the rest. Heat the slide very gently over a spirit lamp or low flame of a bunsen burner for 1 minute (the slide must not be too hot to be placed on the back of the wrist). Squash the apex under a cover glass, making sure the cells are well dispersed. Examine under high power for stages of mitosis, as illustrated by a set of photographs or slides.

        An alternative method of staining is to place the root tips in acetic alcohol 2–3 weeks before they are needed, and add enough aceto-orcein to give a distinct red coloration to the liquid. The chromosomes absorb the stain gradually, and the root tips can be removed from the liquid and squashed in 5% glycerol, without first hydrolysing the tissue. Prolonged fixation loosens the cells.

        Apices kept for 6–8 weeks in this way have given very distinctly stained nuclei, and it is worthwhile storing excess apices in fixative/stain.

(ii) Growth of an individual.

    a) Use an auxanometer to show the growth of a shoot as in Fig. 25 The beam magnifies the actual growth which can be worked out by the ratio of the distance ab:bc; here 1:6.

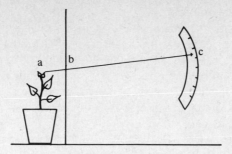

Fig. 25 The rate of growth of a shoot indicated by an auxamometer

b) Using squared paper, follow the growth pattern of a new leaf opening on a tree or shrub. Outline the leaf at daily intervals, and plot a graph as shown in Fig. 26.

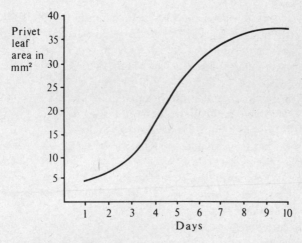

Fig. 26 Graph showing the growth pattern of a leaf

c) Measure the growth of young tadpoles or guppies, by drawing them into a graduated tube. The tube can be calibrated with adhesive tape and Indian ink if commercially made tubes are not available.

(iii) Growth of a population

    a) Place a counted number (about 50) duckweed (*Lemna*) plants in a container of Knop's solution, or place 10 in each of five containers and make the cultures the responsibility of groups of pupils. Count the exact number of fronds. At intervals of a week, count the number of fronds, and plot the numbers as a graph. Artificial (cold) light is necessary in temperate climates where there is little sunshine.

    b) Take a herring ovary (hard roe) and find the weight of it. Weight out 0·5 g portions and count the number of eggs in each. Taking the average, estimate the number of eggs in the whole ovary.

        Assume all will be fertilized, and all fertilized eggs will develop. Estimate the population after five generations, assuming a herring spawns on average five times in its life. Account for the difference between the theoretical population and the actual population.

REPRODUCTION

Invertebrate reproduction and plant reproduction will probably have been dealt with in previous work, when discussing the individual organisms concerned. A revision circus is a good way of drawing together separate items of previous knowledge. The following may be included:

    a) Slide or film loop of division in Amoeba.

    b) Hydra with buds and with ovaries and testes.

    c) An insect having complete metamorphosis.

    d) An insect having incomplete metamorphosis. (Include in c) and d) all stages of the life cycle.)

    e) Stages of metamorphosis in the frog.

    f) Fish—trout eggs (in spring in temperate climates) and guppies or *Tilapia* (Million's fish).

    g) Chick embryology series. Place a fertile chick egg (two if possible) in an incubator at daily intervals for 18 days. This will produce a series of embryonic stages which can be examined together and compared with each other.

    h) Dissection of male and female mammal, labelled by 'flags' or by labels with thread leading from them to the structure concerned, (this is better than trying to demonstrate a dissection to a large class all at the same time. Dissections can be refrigerated for a few days, and can be kept several weeks in the deep freezer or an ice-making compartment.)

i) Mammalian embryo and placenta.

j) Examples of plant propagation by vegetative means.

k) Examples of wind and insect pollinated flowers, pollination mechanisms and fruits and seeds.

A circus as diverse as this will take at least four double lessons. Notes and questions, with instructions for recording, must accompany each example.

SEX EDUCATION

Responsibility for sex education is usually placed with the biology teacher in a school. Whilst the teaching of the facts of human reproduction is an essential part of a biology course, sex education implies a much wider treatment of personal attitudes and moral issues. Excellent material for teaching human reproduction will be found in *Nuffield Secondary Science Theme 3*[8] section 3.2. Even though this topic may have been dealt with in the primary school, a repetition is desirable at the secondary stage. An experienced teacher, especially one with children about the same age as the class concerned, is probably the best person to deal with sex education. It is doubtful whether young teachers are sufficiently certain of their own attitudes and able to be detached enough to discuss objectively with their pupils. In this case, and wherever a teacher is at all uncertain of their ability to give their pupils full and frank answers to questions they may raise, it is better to arrange for an outsider, professionally qualified, to lead discussion. This can be either in lesson time or out of school hours.

Local authorities in Britain usually have school medical officers, or staff from the Family Planning Association or Marriage Guidance Council, qualified and experienced in dealing with school groups. In overseas countries, even in these enlightened days, sex education is much involved in tribal taboos, and it is most unwise for foreign teachers to discuss moral issues with their pupils. However, most of these countries have Family Planning Associations, with qualified nationals of the countries concerned prepared to lead discussion with school groups. It should not be necessary to add that any outside speaker invited to the schools should be approved of, and invited by the Head-teacher concerned.

Biology teachers can prepare their pupils by ensuring they understand the process of human reproduction, and understand the main reasons for the need to limit populations. There are many countries where family planning is seen as a neo-colonialist plot to limit the growth of emergent countries—hence the need to have nationals of the country to explain the reasons for the limitation of populations.

GENETICS

(i) The physical basis of inheritance.

   a) Examine a sequence of photographs of meiotic cell division and slides of human cell nuclei showing homologous chromosomes.

   b) Make aceto-orcein squashes of fifth instar locust testes as described in *Nuffield Biology Text 5*, pp. 38 and 39. The material stains up well by fixing and keeping 2—3 weeks in dilute aceto-orcein stain as described for root tips on p. 110.

   c) Make up a model population of beads or seeds of two colours, and work out the chances of taking two of one colour or one of each colour, with a large number of samples. (Note: always return the 'genes' to the container to keep the 'gene pool' large. Also, if this is not done the numbers of the two 'homozygotes' is bound to be identical.) Relate this model to Mendel's work on a pair of contrasted characters, remembering to point out that Mendel had no knowledge of chromosomes and DNA.

(ii) Living things vary—discontinuous variation.

   a) The ability to taste phenyl thiocarbamide (PTC) is an example of discontinuous variation, but the substance is now thought to be slightly poisonous. It should not be used in schools until further information is available.

   b) Tongue rolling is an inherited ability. The *degree* of rolling seems to improve with practice, though anyone unable to roll their tongue is unable to learn to do so.

(iii) Living things vary—continuous variation.

   a) Count the number of florets on the heads of dandelions or similar plants.

b) Measure the length of a large number of cockroaches or locust imagos.

c) Measure the length of 100 bean seeds.

All the above give a normal distribution curve. Alternatively, the results can be plotted as a histogram, taking groupings as convenient.

Both kinds of variation form the basis on which selection can operate. This in turn brings about the formation of new species— evolution. Excellent material for the continuation of this topic can be found in *'Genetics for O level'* by J.J. Head and N.R. Dennis[12]

EVOLUTION

An understanding of the process of evolution needs prior knowledge of the following:

1. Living things vary.
2. Characteristics are passed on to offspring.
3. More offspring are produced than can survive.
4. Those best suited to their surroundings will survive. The Peppered Moth (*Biston betularia*) is still the best example to use. Illustrative matter and data are readily available. (*Nuffield Biology Text 5* [9])
5. Well adapted organisms have survived at the expense of those less well adapted since life began. The fossil record provides examples, and specific examples are better than a general account. The adaptations of the feet and teeth of the ancestors of the modern horse are suitable examples.
6. Mutation and the part it plays in producing variation can be discussed with the more able groups. An elementary idea of the effects of radiation on mutation is necessary to all in this atomic age.
7. Isolation as a factor in the formation of species has a classic example in the Galapagos finches.
8. It is too rarely emphasized that balanced ecosystems have existed throughout geological time. *The B.S.C.S. Green version* [10] has an chapter on 'Patterns of Life in the Past' which illustrates this point.

FURTHER INFORMATION

In addition to *Nuffield Text and Teachers' Guide 5* [9] *Nuffield Secondary Science Theme 2* [11], *Continuity of Life,* has numerous examples of inheritance and evolution demonstrations and experiments, all tried and tested in schools.

4.5 Microbiology

SAFETY PRECAUTIONS

Pathogenic micro-organisms should not be used in schools. *Bacillus subtilis, Escherichia coli* and *Staphylococcus albus* are permissible and can be obtained as discs for 'seeding' cultures in broth or growing on plates from Oxoid or supply agencies. After use all cultures must be placed in a 10% solution of Lysol, and autoclaved before disposal. Pupils should be trained not to put anything in their mouths, and to wash their hands before and after handling cultures. The danger of contamination is very small, but good habits in handling these organisms should be instilled at an early stage.

'Micro-organisms' are taken to include bacteria and fungi. The approach to their study depends very much on previous work—if pupils have been studying ecology, then soil bacteria will be the starting point. If foods and feeding have just been studied, then the role of bacteria in food spoilage and preservation could be the starting point. Thus, the following experiments are not intended to be necessarily followed in the sequence given.

WHAT ARE BACTERIA?

Leave a piece of potato or a few pea or bean seeds in water in a warm place for 4—5 days. There will be abundant growth of bacteria. Examine some of the bacterial suspension as follows:

a) Under high power, unstained but with a cover glass.

b) Using an inoculating loop (nichrome wire fused into a glass rod, as shown in Fig. 27) mix a loopful of the bacterial culture with a similar quantity of Indian ink on a clean microscope slide. Spread

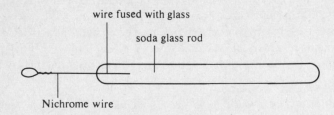

Fig. 27 An inoculating loop

out the liquid to a thin film, and allow it to dry. Pass the slide *quickly* two or three times through a flame to fix the bacteria. Examine under oil immersion if possible, or use high power. The bacteria are seen as unstained, colourless structures amongst the carbon particles of the Indian ink.

c) Make a smear of bacteria as above, omitting the Indian ink. After fixing, cover the smear with methylene blue, eosin or safranin to stain the bacteria, leaving the stain for 2—3 minutes. Rinse off excess stain under a tap, and examine using oil immersion.

WHERE ARE BACTERIA FOUND?

Prepare sterile nutrient agar plates or slopes:

Dissolve agar tablets and nutrient broth tablets in water in the quantities shown. Tablets are obtainable from supply agencies or direct from Oxoid Ltd. Alternatively, dissolve in water:

> 10 g beef extract (any domestic kind)
> 10 g peptone
> 5 g sodium chloride
> 1 litre water

Adjust pH to 7·5 with sodium bicarbonate. Heat below boiling point until all ingredients are dissolved and then filter.

To the resulting nutrient broth add 1·5 g agar per 100ml. and heat at 45—50°C until the agar is melted. A thermostatic water bath is useful for this process. When the agar has dissolved, place 10ml of the liquid in McCartney bottles (small screw top jars, all parts being heat resistant), and sterilize in a pressure cooker or autoclave at 15lbs/20 minutes. The screw tops should be loose before sterilization, and tightened when still hot. In practice, it is best to turn the tops to the limit of the thread, and then make half a turn back to loosen.

If test tube slopes are required, the culture medium can be sterilized in the tubes, but they must be covered in metal foil or two layers of brown paper firmly tied on to prevent steam condensing inside the tubes and diluting the medium.

Pouring plates

Use packs of sterile disposable Petri dishes, or bake glass dishes in an oven at about 250 °C. Each dish should be individually wrapped in wax paper before sterilizing. Melt the agar medium in the closed tubes in a water bath at 45 °C, loosening the caps slightly first.

Unwrap petri dishes one by one as required, and pour the hot medium quickly as shown below. The tube cap is conveniently removed by holding it by the little finger and palm of the left hand, and unscrewing *the tube* with the right hand. The left hand is used to lift the petri dish lid. Rotate the dish gently to spread the medium evenly, and invert as soon as the medium solidifies.

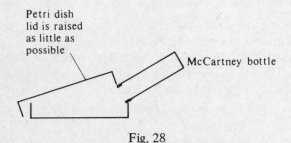

Petri dish lid is raised as little as possible

McCartney bottle

Fig. 28

Once set, a process taking ten minutes or so, the plates can be infected in a variety of ways suggested by the class. For example, sweep dust from a bench over one plate, place one open in the laboratory for half an hour, and another for the same length of time outside. Catch a house-fly and place it on a plate. A control must be left, to test the sterility of the medium. Incubate all cultures and the control at 37 °C.

THE FOOD OF SOME BACTERIA

a) Make up nutrient agar as described above, but add 0·5g milk powder per 100ml liquid. Streak a loopful of sour milk over the plate. The lactobacilli feed off the milk casein, and their colonies thus have a clear area round them after 2–3 days incubation at 37°C.

b) Make up nutrient agar, but use 1% starch solution in place of water in the recipe given above for nutrient agar. Streak bacteria, from a potato or bean 'culture' over the plate. After 2–3 days incubation, flood the plate with iodine solution. Where starch remains, there will be the usual blue colour of the starch/iodine compound. Where bacteria have utilized the starch, there will be a clear area. Avoid using a high concentration of iodine in the solution. A very pale brown colour gives the best results.

Streaking a plate
1. Flame a nichrome wire loop, and take up a loopful of culture.
2. Open a plate by raising the lid to about 45° with the left hand. Place the drop of culture at point A on the diagram.

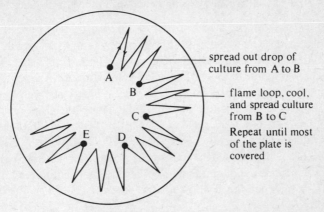

Fig. 29   Streaking a plate.

3. Flame the loop, and cool it by placing it momentarily on the edge of the agar plate. Now use the loop to spread the drop of bacterial culture, as shown in the diagram.
4. Flame the loop again, and repeat the process of spreading the bacteria, until most of the dish has been covered. It is essential to flame the loop between each 'spreading' process, otherwise separate colonies will not be distinguishable.

BACTERIA IN MILK
Note: the pasteurization process kills most pathogenic bacteria—it does not kill all bacteria. Thus, newly pasteurized milk can be expected to show some bacterial colonies in the following experiment
   a) Take samples of milk which have been pasteurised, sterilized by boiling, sterilized by ultra heat treatment, and raw milk. Streak each over nutrient agar, and leave one plate as a control. Compare the bacterial growth after incubation.
   b) Take samples of milk as above, in a set of test tubes in a water bath at 37 °C. Add a resazurin tablet, or 1ml 5% methylene blue

to each tube. (In the case of resazurin, protect the tubes from light).

Note the time taken for the resazurin to change to a pink colour, or for the methylene blue to be decolourized. The faster rate of decolourization means a greater number of bacteria.

CULTURING MOULDS

a) Place a piece of home made bread (many commercial breads contain artificial preservatives) between a pair of petri dishes, keeping the bread moist. In a warm place, mould colonies develop in a few days. It helps to wipe the slice of bread over one of the laboratory benches, to collect dust and hence fungal spores.

b) Inoculate a starch/agar plate with a little of the mould colonies. Growth is more readily observed, especially at the outer circumference of the growing colony. (Use a binocular microscope)

Show the use of starch by flooding the plate with iodine solution, when the mould colony is covering about half the plate area.

ANTIBIOTICS

Flood a plate with a culture of B. subtilis, prepared according to the instructions supplied with the seeding discs. Draw off the excess liquid with a pipette. Place a penicillin disc at the centre of the plate and incubate the culture. Penicillin diffuses from the disc into the surrounding medium, and inhibits growth of the bacterium.

Alternatively, some of the mould colonies growing on the breadmould culture will be *Penicillium.* Culture a colony on nutrient agar, and when the colony is about 2cm in diameter, flood the plate with a culture of B. subtilis.

If culture discs cannot be obtained, experiment with potato or bean bacterial cultures and the mould colonies which appear on bread and fruits.

DECOMPOSING ACTION OF MOULDS AND BACTERIA

The role of bacteria and fungi in the soil is often overlooked, and may be dealt with in part of the course not related to microbiology. Decomposers are as important in an ecosystem as the producers and consumers usually studied in great detail, in that they enable the re-

circulation of minerals. There should be less concentration on the
nitrogen cycle and closer attention to the circulation of *all* inorganic
compounds by the action of decomposers.

a) The moulds and bacteria in soil.

Mix 5ml soil with 10ml water. Shake well, allow to settle, and
streak some of the liquid over nutrient agar plates.
Incubate at 37 °C for 2–3 days.

b) Decay of cellulose films.

Wrap a 4 X 2cm strip of cellulose round a microscope slide,
holding the ends with thread or rubber bands. Bury the slides in
a pot of damp, fresh soil in the laboratory, or in the garden. In the
latter case, tie a string to each slide to remain above ground level
for location of the slide. Examine the films after about a week,
using a monocular microscope and 100X magnification. Fungi
and actinomycetes will be seen, and bacteria can be observed under
high power. Re-bury the slides for a further two weeks, keeping
the soil damp. Re-examination will show decay of the cellulose.
Note: many cellulose films used in wrappings are covered in a
thin layer of polythene. Supply agencies stock pure cellulose,
though it is worth experimenting with cellophane wrappings.

FURTHER WORK

This work leads on to:

a) The biology of food preservation by preventing the growth of
bacteria and moulds.

b) The control of disease—immunity, antibiotics.

c) Soil studies in connection with ecology.

d) Industrial uses of micro-organisms—chemical, tea, coffee, leather
industries.

FURTHER INFORMATION

Nuffield Biology Teachers' Guide II [5] and the *B.S.C.S. Laboratory
Block 'Microbes: their growth, nutrition and interaction'* [6] . Both have
additional experimental work.

4.6 Cell structure and the physico-chemical properties of cytoplasm.

THE CELLULAR STRUCTURE OF ORGANISMS

(i) Simple animal cells

Cells from the lining of the cheek are easily removed with a clean spatula or finger nail. Placed in dilute iodine or methylene blue solution on a slide and examined under low power, the nucleus and cytoplasm can be clearly seen.

(ii) Simple plant cells

A single moss leaf, or leaf of a water plant such as *Elodea* or *Hydrilla* shows typical chloroplast containing cells, without any staining. The tissue is simply mounted in dilute glycerine and examined under low power. Onion or garlic leaf epidermis can be easily detached from the food-storing leaves of the bulb, and shows plant cells without chloroplasts.

(iii) Specialized cells

   a) Conducting cells from plants—root tips half to one centimetre long
      from onion or garlic bulbs can be observed by squashing the tissue
      on a microscope slide. Gentle heating in dilute hydrochloric acid
      facilitates separation of the cells. Spirally thickened xylem is easily
      distinguishable.

   b) Muscle cells—striated muscle cells, actually occurring as a syncitium,
      can be seen in any red meat teased out on a microscope slide. Insect
      muscle tissue is especially easy to observe, and it is worthwhile
      mounting such tissue when dissecting large insects such as cockroaches
      and locusts.

PROPERTIES OF PROTOPLASM

(i) Living tissue contains enzymes

   a) *Catalase activity*
      Catalase breaks down hydrogen peroxide into oxygen and water.
      It occurs in most living tissue, and can be simply tested for by
      adding 10 vol. hydrogen peroxide to a variety of materials, living
      and non-living. Effervescence indicates the presence of the enzyme.
      Suitable materials are fresh meat or liver, root vegetables, ground
      leaf material (simply pulped in a mortar and pestle), and a few
      non-living materials such as cork, plastic, dried bone, shell etc.

b) *Digestive enzymes*

The action of saliva on a 1% colloidal starch solution is to change the starch to a reducing sugar, maltose. The effect can be observed by testing a sample from a mixture of starch and saliva for the presence of reducing sugar incubating the mixture at 35 °C for half an hour, and re-testing for reducing sugars. Either Fehling's or Benedict's solution can be used for the sugar test. Other digestive enzymes can be extracted from the intestine of any animal freshly filled for dissection. Open up a little of the intestine, near the stomach. Pipette in a few cm^3 of Ringer and draw out the resulting mixture of intestinal juices with a pipette or hypodermic syringe. The mixture dissolves 1 mm cubes of coagulated egg white, and dissolves the gelatine layer off photographic film. The contents of the cockroach gut has a similar effect.

(ii) The cell membrane

The cell membrane or plasma-membrane retains the cell contents whilst the cell is alive. It is semi-permeable and important in retaining turgidity in plants.

a) *Death point of cells*

Any coloured plant material—washed beetroot or flower petals—shows that the cell contents escape when the protoplasm is killed by heat. Place the material in water in a test tube, together with a thermometer. Set up a similar tube as a control. Heat up the experiment tube in a water bath, noting the temperature at which the coloured cell contents begin to escape.

b) *Turgidity in cells*

Cut equal cylinders of potato or similar tuber with a cork borer. Place a cylinder in distilled water, in 1%, 5%, 10%, and 20% salt solution. Examine all the cylinders after ten minutes. Place them in labelled tubes of distilled water, and see which recover their turgidity.

Observation of plasmolysis in a single cell is best observed on moss leaves or water plant leaves.

c) *Transport of water by osmosis*

Place the root hair region of seedlings such as Mung beans (Bengal green gram) in water coloured with eosin. In about half an hour the vascular tissue can be seen to be stained red.

d) *Osmosis using egg membrane*

Dissolve the shells off two equal sized eggs by immersing in dilute hydrochloric acid. Place one egg in 5% sugar solution, the other in distilled water. Note the difference in size after a few hours. Egg membrane makes a good substitute for cellophane or visking tubing in standard osmosis demonstrations.

e) *Osmosis as the movement of small molecules*

Set up two sets of apparatus as shown in Fig. 30. In A the visking tubing contains 1% colloidal starch solution, and the beaker contains dilute iodine solution. In B the position of the two solutions is reversed. The iodine is able to pass through the tubing and shows the usual blue/black colouration.

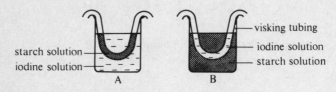

Fig. 30 To show osmosis as the movement of small molecules

(iii) The cell nucleus and division
See p. 110 'Growth of a cell'.

Bibliography

1. Nuffield Biology Text IV, Living things in action. Longman/Penguin 1966.
2. Nuffield Biology Text III, The maintainence of life. Longman/Penguin 1966.
3. Food Resources, Convential and Novel. Pirie. Penguin Books 1969.
4. Nuffield Secondary Science: Theme 4, Harnessing Energy. Longman 1971.
5. Nuffield Biology Teachers' Guide II, Life and living processes. Longman/Penguin 1966.
6. Microbes: their growth, nutrition and interaction. A.J. Sussman. B.S.C.S. D.C. Heath and Co., Boston, U.S.A.

7. The Development Puzzle.
   Voluntary Committee on Overseas Aid, 69 Victoria Street, London SW1.

8. Nuffield Secondary Science: Theme 3, Biology of Man. Longman 1971.

9. Nuffield Biology Text V, The perpetuation of life. Longman/Penguin 1967.

10. High School Biology. B.S.C.S. Rand McNally, U.S.A. 1963.

11. Nuffield Secondary Science: Theme 2 Continuity of Life. Longman 1971.

12. Genetics for O level. J.J. Head and N.R. Dennis. Oliver & Boyd 1968.